Investing In
Stocks For Beginners

The Knowledge Needed to Get Started and Avoid Rookie Mistakes

Maxx Waring

Contents

Section 1: Introduction

This book is not going to tell you how to become a millionaire in a day, month, or year. But it will show you how easily anyone in the United States can become a millionaire if they can just live long enough. If there was one piece of advice I would give you, it would be to read. Just about everything I write in this book I have learned from reading. Well, I should say reading and listening to Warren Buffett and Charlie Munger, two of the smartest humans on this planet. They would advise we start by looking at the S&P 500, and so we shall:

S&P 500

The easiest and safest way to become a millionaire is to invest into the S&P 500. The S&P 500 is just a collection of the 500 biggest U.S Companies, so investing here you will own a part of the majority of U.S Businesses. A very critical thing to know is that buying stock is buying a share of that company. You become a partial owner. Most people do not understand that fact, even a lot of stock traders. You are not buying a little symbol that moves up and down; you are buying a piece of a business, hopefully a wonderful business. So, by investing in the S&P 500, you become an owner of 500 of the biggest businesses in the U.S.

In the last 100 years the S&P 500 has averaged about 10% growth per year after dividends. Let us say you graduate high school at 18 and start working at McDonald's. You decide you want to do the smart thing and invest your money. So, you be frugal and limit your alcohol, cannabis, other drug, and shopping/entertainment spending, and you save 100 dollars each month. I believe most people with a full-time job can find $100 dollars a month to save.

If you put that $100.00 per month into the S&P 500, with an average of 10% growth per year, for the next 47 years—from age 18 to the age of 65—you would now have over a million dollars! $1,046,369.82 to be exact. The wonderful thing about compound interest is, as you pile up more money, your money grows faster. It is exponential growth. Imagine a snowball rolling down a hill forever. It is going to start off small, but it will continue to double and double in size as it moves down this hill; soon it will be the size of a house. So, after 47 years you have 1 Million dollars. A 10 percent growth rate is going to double your money about every 7 years. Thus, even if you stop contributing 100 dollars per month after you turn 65, in 7 more years you will have 2 Million dollars, 7 more years 4 Million Dollars, and so on. By age 79 you could have 4 Million dollars by only investing $100 dollars a month for 47 Years, then just sitting back and watching your money grow. Compound interest truly is the 8th wonder of the world.

Let us compare this growth to if you just put $100/month away in a bank, or under your mattress, for 47 years. All you would have then is $56,400! That is almost 1 Million dollars less than what you get if you invest! On top of that, without putting more money into the S&P 500, your money is going to continue to grow. By age 79 you would have $4 Million from investing and your money under your mattress will still be $56,400. After all that time inflation would've eaten away a lot of that $56,400 spending power, but that conversation is for another day.

You might say well it will not be worth it because I can never take it out; I want to spend the money while I am alive. Again, it is only 100 dollars a month—that is not a huge sacrifice when you think about all the items you spend money on every month. Anyway, if you wait until 65 to touch your 1 million dollars, at that point you could take out $500,000 and buy whatever you wanted. It could be a house, car, boat, grandkids' college, kids' mortgage; whatever your heart desires. You would still have $500,000 in the S&P 500, and 7 years later you would be back up to a million dollars if it averaged 10% a year.

A great way to invest in the S&P 500 is through retirement account. The Roth IRA is a great retirement option because it is tax free as long as you hold the account until you are at least 59.5 years old. There are income limits to this. For one, you can only put earned income into a Roth IRA; if you did not earn any money for the year, you cannot deposit money into a Roth IRA. Secondly, there is a maximum deposit of $6,000 per year. And finally, if you make more than $124,000 you cannot contribute to a Roth IRA. If you are married and file jointly, your maximum contribution goes up to $12,000 and your income limit goes up to $196,000. You can create a Roth IRA with most banks.

Once you have either a brokerage account or an IRA, you can invest in the S&P 500. You can invest by either putting your money in a mutual fund or an ETF that mirrors the S&P 500. I like Vanguard's ETF (VOO). But whichever you choose, just make sure they have a low Expense ratio—a fancy word for how much they charge you.

There is a decent chance the S&P 500 does not average 10% for the next 47 years. There is a tiny chance it does better, but I would guess it might do a little worse. Even so, the S&P 500 is going to be a solid investment. The American economy is going to go through rough patches, but the American economy is very strong regardless of whoever the President is and whatever they are saying on TV.

Here is a table of what your investment will look like at different average interest rates and if you contributed $100.00 per month. (All Values are rounded down to the nearest whole number).

Values are from - https://www.investor.gov/financial-tools-calculators/calculators/compound-interest-calculator
(U.S Securities and Exchange Commission, n.d.)

Yrs	5%	6%	7%	8%	9%	10%	11%	12%
10	$15,093	$15,816	$16,579	$17,383	$18,231	$19,124	$20,066	$21,058
20	$39,679	$44,142	$49,194	$54,914	$61,392	$68,730	$77,043	$86,462
30	$79,726	$94,869	$113,352	$135,939	$163,569	$197,392	$238,825	$289,599
40	$144,959	$185,714	$239,562	$310,867	$405,458	$531,111	$698,191	$920,509
47	$213,743	$289,318	$395,069	$543,480	$752,235	$1,046,369	$1,461,296	$2,047,060
50	$251,217	$348,403	$487,834	$688,524	$978,100	$1,396,690	$2,002,525	$2,880,021
60	$424,300	$639,753	$976,224	$1,503,855	$2,333,750	$3,641,779	$5,706,079	$8,965,969
75	$907,984	$1,561,138	$2,723,588	$4,803,067	$8,535,878	$15,250,744	$27,342,532	$49,120,558
100	$3,132,030	$6,788,041	$14,857,994	$32,981,418	$73,707,210	$165,355,348	$371,598,275	$835,212,657

The values multiply evenly if you add more money each month. For example, if you invested $200 a month at 5% for 10 years, you would just multiply $15,093 by 2 and would have $30,186. If you invested $500 a month at 12% for 100 years you would multiply $835,212,657 by 5 and have over 4 Billion dollars: $4,176,063,285.

Observe on the table that each percentage point adds a lot of value in the long term. This is why you need to be very careful about how much advisors charge you for their services. The difference between 12% and 11% is only 1% but over 100 years the difference is over $460 Million investing only $100 a month.

Over the next 40-50 years, I think expecting somewhere between 5% and 11% is reasonable if you are investing a certain amount monthly. If you were to invest a giant lump sum at the end of a bull market (a bull market is when stocks have gone up significantly over a period of time), then you could maybe do a little worse than 5%. But if you are investing monthly, I highly doubt it will be less than 5%. I also highly doubt it will be more than 10%. I would guess the return over the next 50 years in the S&P 500 will be between 6% and 10%, hopefully closer to the 10% it has returned over the last 100 years. These returns are not going to be consistent every year, some years the S&P 500 might lose 20-30% or more but you are investing for the long haul and the year-to-year swings shouldn't bother you. You are interested in the average return per year.

If you decide not to invest in the S&P 500 and let an advisor manage your money, you need to watch their performance after all taxes, fees, and any other expenses and see how it compares to the S&P 500. Compare on a 3, 5, and 10 years average basis. If your advisor returns less than the S&P 500 (which most advisors and hedge funds do, due to fees), they are stealing your money. Anyone can mindlessly be average and get the returns of the S&P 500;

do not pay someone to underperform the market. A lot of people pay a lot of money for underperformance.

Now you know how easy it is to become a millionaire with enough time. If that sounds good to you and you want to outperform most money managers with little to no effort and get the average of American businesses, then there is no need to read on. However, if you want to do better than average and try to get into the range of 10%-25% a year, you need to be willing to spend considerable time reading and thinking. I doubt anyone will average more than 20% a year for their career—that's Warren Buffett's status at Berkshire Hathaway, the greatest of all time. His performance would be closer to 30% or higher, but it is much harder to compound money when you have hundreds of billions of dollars.

Again, if average sounds good to you quit reading. If you want to try for better than average, continue reading this book, and I will go on to show you how to avoid my stupid mistakes.

Reading

If you are going to beat the market over a lifetime, you are going to spend thousands of hours reading books, annual reports, and any other news and information about companies. 20% a year might not sound very hard, but I would guess that fewer than 1% of people will be able to do it. However, it can be very rewarding financially; $500 a month with a 20% yearly return will be about $272 Million in 50 years. In the Further Reading section at the end of this book, I have provided a list of materials I recommend reading if you are going to attempt to buy your own stocks.

If the prospect of consistent reading seems daunting, do not worry; I hated reading until after high school and finally found books I enjoyed. Just start by reading a few pages a day and working your way up to a few hours a day. Your knowledge will really add up like compound interest. Reading is the key to being a good investor. I would also suggest reading anything you are interested in, not just books on investing.

> "In my whole life, I have known no wise people (over a broad subject matter area) who did not read all the time—none, zero. You would be amazed at how much Warren reads—and at how much I read. My children laugh at me. They think I'm a book with a couple of legs sticking out." – Charlie Munger (Munger, 2006, p. xx)

On top of reading, I would highly recommend listening to Berkshire Hathaway's Annual meetings. CNBC has all of these since 1994 on their website titled *The Buffett Archives*. I have listened to all these meetings and you will gain a wide range of insights on many topics.

Section 2: Investing Basics

Most people will try to overcomplicate investing to make it seem like only an elite few are capable of investing. But investing is simple. It is not easy, but it is simple. In this section I will go over some basic investing ideas and vocabulary.

Imagine being a kid and there is a very popular lemonade stand in your neighborhood. There is always a line of people and the money is just pouring in. One day you get talking to the kids running the lemonade stand and tell them you want to become partners with them. They say great, for 50 dollars you can own half of the business, entitling you to half the profits and or half the losses of this business. At first you are thinking great I am going to make a fortune. However, after a week of costumers lined up down the street, your partners say you are going to need to put up 5 dollars for the needed inventory for the coming week. You go on to realize that this lemonade stand does not make a profit. Rather, they are selling the lemonade too cheap. On top of that, your partners have been upgrading the stand with cooler decorations and they mysteriously both have brand new bikes. So, although this business was popular, and was indeed busy everyday with sales, they were not profiting any money at all. They were actually losing money with unnecessary upgrades/costs and high personal salaries. It was a "popular" business, but **a poor investment.** Not every shiny new business that appears great is a good investment—even if you love their product.

This misapprehension is a common mistake investors make. People put money into stocks without looking at the business and their profits. They then unknowingly invest into companies that lose millions of dollars a day. Meanwhile the CEO and other high-up employees are making millions, sometimes even billions, and riding around on their yachts.

It is natural to get excited about a company you like and jump into it. If you have done this, it's okay, I have too. That is what happens before we learn. And hey, you are reading this now and will not make that mistake again. In fact, before I took time to educate myself, I was dumb enough to put my money into **eight** companies like this. This was before I read *The Intelligent Investor*. They all ended in a loss and one went totally bankrupt while I owned it. I lost about 25% of my net worth. Good thing I learned this lesson in college when I did not have very much money to lose. Do not buy a stock because you heard it was the "hot" stock. Do not buy a stock just because you like or use their product. Only buy a stock because it is a good investment. Period.

Alright, now for some bullet point basics:

Bullet Point Basics

- The most basic lesson needed to invest in the stock market is that you are not putting your money into a symbol that moves up and down; you are buying a piece of a business. Most people, and even a lot of stock traders, do not understand this concept: "In order to value the stock, you must value the business." – Charlie Munger (*ValueQuotes — Investment masters class*, n.d.)

- You want to invest in companies that make a profit, or you are certain they will make a profit soon. This sounds obvious. However, many people invest in companies that lose billions a year with no chance at a turnaround.

- When buying a stock or a company you need to think about what it is going to look like 5, 10, 15, 20 years down the road. You are not buying a company to sell it 2 months later; you are investing in the company for the long haul. If you are not willing to own a stock for 10 years, do not even think about owning it for 10 minutes.

- You need to be able to think for yourself. Do not listen to what you read on the internet or see on TV. I bought those eight bad companies because I had read online that they were a "hot" stock to buy. Well, it was not hot losing money.

- The price of a stock has **nothing** to do with the business or the business's value. A 10-billion-dollar company could sell for $2.00/share and a 10-Million-dollar company could sell for $10,000/share. Berkshire Hathaway, a good investment, can sell for

$351,900/share. Compare this to the many extremely terrible and overvalued investments that sell for $0.01/share. The price of a stock is irrelevant.

- The company's **market capitalization (market cap) or market value** is what matters. The market cap is what the entire company is currently selling for in the stock market. The market cap is simply the number of shares the company has multiplied by the price of each share. For example, Apple has 16.82 Billion shares outstanding. Apple's stock price is currently at $142.92. Simply multiply 16.82 Billion shares by the stock price of $142.92/share and get 2.4 Trillion Dollars. Apple is currently selling for 2.4 trillion.

- When deciding to invest in a company you want to imagine you are paying for the entire business. Looking at Apple, you need to come up with the answer to "Is Apple worth $2.4 Trillion?" If you think the company is worth less than that $2.4 trillion, then do not invest. If you think it is worth more than $2.4 Trillion, you can invest in it. If you cannot figure out how much the company is worth, then you do not invest in it. Figuring out the value of a business is the difficult part of investing.

- The value of a business is how much cash the company will produce from today to judgment day. (We will talk more about this later).

- Companies can do **three things** with the cash they produce: They can either pay a dividend, buy back shares, or retain earnings and build a more competitive and profitable business.

- **Dividends** are the cash the company pays you. If you had 100 shares of a company and they paid $1.00 per share a year in dividends, then you would receive $100.00 a year in dividends.

- **Dividend Yield** is the percentage return a year from dividends. Looking at the previous example, if the price of the stock were at $100.00/share, then the dividend yield would be 1%. $1 a share in dividends divided by $100 a share equals 0.01 or 1.00%. If the stock were selling for $10, the yield would be 10%—$1 a share in dividends divided by $10 for the price of the stock is 0.10 or 10%.

- **Repurchasing/issuing Shares** – The dynamic between repurchasing and issuing shares is an important concept to understand because it directly affects your interest in the company. The number of shares a company has outstanding is simply the number of shares people in the world own of this company. The company can decide to buy back these shares, issue shares, or do neither. If your company is buying back shares, this is very good for shareholders if purchased at the right price. For example, if you own 10 shares of a company that has 100 shares, you own 10% of the company and are entitled to 10% of the company's profits. If the company repurchases 10 shares or 10% of the company, you now own 10 shares out of 90; thus, you now own 11.11 % of the company and their profits. Over time, this process can make a huge difference on the return of your investment. On the other hand, if your company is issuing shares, they are literally giving away your share of the company. Let us use the same example except this time the company issues 10 more shares or 10% more. Now instead of owning 10% of the company, you own 10 shares of a company with 110 shares. 10 shares out of 110 shares means that you now only own 9.09% of your company. If your company is issuing more shares, they better have a good reason for it and profits better be increasing more than the percentage of shares they are issuing a year. (There is probably not a good reason). Companies issue shares when they are in desperate need for cash. If they can't pay the bills, they will issue shares and use the cash to pay off debt. However, this dilutes your ownership in the company. Also companies issue shares as a way to pay management without it showing up on the income statement. Obviously paying CEO's by issuing shares is an expense and need to be counted in your calculation. One of the only reasons issuing a stock is a good thing is if your company is extremely overvalued in the market and the company can use that cash effectively. You do not want your company to give away your share!

- **Retained Earnings** are the cash the company chooses not to distribute to shareholders, instead using it to build a more competitive and profitable business. If the company continually retains earnings but does not or cannot build a better business, then you have a problem. In this case, you would want the business to pay all excess cash and profits back to you in dividends or buybacks.

- **Margin of error** is crucial. You want a big margin of safety. If Apple is selling for $2.4 Trillion (Market Cap) and you think Apple is worth somewhere between $2.4 Trillion and $2.5 Trillion, this is a small margin of safety. A few years ago, Apple was selling for $500 Billion. At that time, if you thought it was worth somewhere between $2 Trillion and $3 Trillion, then this would be a large margin of safety.

- **Stocks become less risky as the price of the stock goes down**. Stocks are riskier as their prices are going up. This is sometimes hard for people to understand, but you should want stock prices to go down so you can buy the same companies at a better price.

- **The stock market is irrational**. Imagine the stock market as an extremely emotional man named Mr. Market. Mr. Market comes to you 5 days a week for 6.5 hours a day all year round. He offers you instant prices on thousands of companies, any public company you want. The nice thing about Mr. Market is he does not care if you ever buy or sell any stocks, he will come back the next day and start the whole process over. Anyway, being the emotional fellow he is, the prices he offers for the same companies are going to be very different day to day and especially after months and years. When times are good, Mr. Market can see nothing wrong with the world and his prices for businesses are going to rise dramatically. Other times, Mr. Market is going to get really depressed and fear the world is falling apart; his prices are going to sink and he will be willing to give away great companies for bargains.

- **The Stock market is there to serve you, not instruct you.** Do not let Mr. Market tempt you into buying companies that are too expensive and do not let him tempt you to sell companies when he thinks the world is ending.

- **Assets** are any item a company has that gives the company value. Assets can include cash, inventory, property, investments, and many other items.

- **Liabilities** are everything the company owes to others. Liabilities can include loans, money owed to suppliers, legal fees, etc.

- **Book Value** consists of all assets on a company's balance sheet subtracted by the liabilities. Example: Apple has $324 Billion in Assets and $259 Billion in liabilities. $324 Billion minus $259 Billion equals $65 Billion. Thus, Apple's Book Value is $65 Billion.

- **Shareholder Equity** – If you are looking on a balance sheet, book value would be referred to as shareholder equity. Thus, like book value, shareholder equity is equal to Assets minus Liabilities.

- **Book Value per share** is just the Book Value divided by the number of shares. For example, Apple's Book Value is $65 Billion and the number of shares is 16.82 Billion. Book Value per share is 65 Billion divided by 16.82 Billion to get $3.86 per share. Whenever you want to find the per share value just divide the value by the number of shares. Pretty straightforward.

- **Price to Book Ratio (PB)** is the number of times the book value is multiplied to equal the market cap of the stock, which gives you the ratio.
  For example: Apple is currently selling for $2.4 Trillion and its book value is currently $65 Billion. To find the Price to Book Value (PB) simply take 2.4 Trillion and divide it by 65 billion and get 36.92. So, currently Apple is selling for 36.92 times higher than its book value. The PB Ratio is 36.92.

- **Revenue** is the total amount of sales of the company's products or services.

- **Expenses** are all the costs of running the business, such as the cost of the revenue, labor, rent, research, and development—anything that costs the company money.

- **Operating income** is the company's profit after running the day-to-day business.

- **Net income**, also known as **earnings**, is the profit after everything is considered including taxes.

- **Earnings per share** is the company's Net Income divided by the number of shares the company has. Example: Apple has $55 Billion in earnings and 16.82 Billion shares. Take $55 Billion and divide it by 16.82 Billion shares and get $3.27 earnings per share.

- **Stock Split** – A stock split does nothing to change the value of a company, but most people get excited when a company stock splits. If a company is selling for $100 a share and it splits 1 for 4, now the same exact company is selling for $25 a share. The market cap remains the same; everything about the company remains the same except the number of shares multiplies by 4. If you had 100 shares before the split, you now have 400 shares after. It is like cutting a pizza into more slices, the size of the pizza has not changed, just the number of slices.

- **Compound annual growth rate (CAGR)** – The average yearly return on an investment. It is not as easy as just taking the total percent return and dividing it by the number of years. For example, if you invested $10,000 into a company and after 10 years your total grows to $20,000, you gained $10,000 dollars; this would be a 100% gain. If you divided 100% by 10 years you would get 10% a year, but that does not account for compound interest. The compounded annual growth rate would be 7.18%. If you had invested $10,000 and had a 10% CAGR for 10 Years, you would now have $25,937.42—a difference of almost $6,000 dollars. This is the beauty of compound interest: a small difference can make a huge impact on your investments, **which is why you need to be very careful if your financial advisor is charging high fees**.

- **Bonds** – Bonds are fixed rate investments issued by either the government or companies.
Here is an example: If you bought a $10,000 bond that yields 10% for 10 years, upfront you pay $10,000 for this bond. Over the next 10 years this bond is going to pay you 10% of 10,000, which is $1,000 each year, usually 6 months apart so $500 twice a year. After 10 years the bond expires, and you get your initial investment of $10,000 back. So, after 10 years you received $10,000 in payments and got your initial $10,000. So, you are left with $20,000. Looking back at our last example we can see this is a CAGR of not 10% but 7.18%. That is still a very solid return. The way you can lose in an investment like this is if the company or government that issues the bond goes bankrupt. In that case you would have lost all your investment but would get to keep any money they distributed before bankruptcy. Again, it is a little more complicated than this because you can buy a bond for a discount or premium, and people use fancy terms. But the above gives us a decent understanding of bonds for beginners.

- **Coupon-** Is the rate the bond will pay you yearly. In the last example the $10,000 bond yielded 10% a year. This is a coupon rate of 10%.

- **Treasury Bonds** – These are issued by the U.S government and considered the safest form of investment for the simple fact that it is the United States. Like a Lannister always pays its debts. Currently the 10 yr. treasury rate is 1.09% which is very low historically. In the early 80s the treasury rate was over 14%. Typically, the longer the duration of the bond the higher the yield. The 30 yr. treasury rate is usually higher than the 10 yr.

- **An important point to remember is dishonest managers and accountants can make a company's income look a lot better than it is.**

PE Ratio/Earnings Yield

Okay let's talk about price-to-earnings now. Also known as a PE Ratio. This is the number of times the earnings (or Net income) are multiplied to get to the Market Value of the stock. Say the market cap or market value of Apple was $550 Billion, with $55 Billion in Net Income/earnings in 2019; the PE Ratio would be 10. ($55 Billion x 10 PE = $550 Billion).

The lower the PE Ratio, the cheaper the stock is selling for compared to earnings. The higher the PE ratio, the lower the current earnings are compared to the price at which you are buying the company. In our last example, Apple was selling for $550 Billion with earnings of $55 Billion; this is a PE ratio of 10. Now to find the **earnings yield** take $55 Billion and divide it by $550 Billion you will get .10, which is 10%. This means that at $550 Billion you are getting a 10% earnings yield. You might think of this as a return on your investment, even though the earnings yield does not guarantee that 10% will be your return on this investment. The company must return this net income to investors in either dividends, repurchasing shares, or retaining earnings to make the company more competitive and profitable. Making an investment is much more complicated than just looking at PE ratios to determine what your return on an investment will be. The PE ratio alone cannot tell us if the company is a good investment, but again this book is for beginners. And remember that CEOs and accountants can make 1 quarter or even 1 year's worth of financial statements look a lot better than they really are—eventually the truth always comes out.

If Apple were selling for $2.4 Trillion but still only earning $55 Billion a year, we can find the company's PE ratio by dividing the price by the earnings. 2.4 Trillion divided by 55 Billion is 43.6. So, the PE ratio is 43.6. To find your return or earnings yield on this investment, you would just do the inverse. Take 55 Billion and divide it by 2.4 Trillion to get .023, which is 2.3%. If we are given a choice between these two options, it is clearly better to invest in Apple when it is selling for $550 Billion—a 10% return or earnings yield—than when it was selling for $2.4 Trillion, a mere 2.3% return.

Imagine you found a house you loved and it was selling for $200,000. Now, after a week goes by you contact the real estate agent, and they inform you that the price has changed. Would you rather the price go up or down? Obviously, you would want the price to decrease so you could buy the same great house for a lesser price. However, a lot of investors do not understand this; most people would rather have the stock market moving up than down, but it is the same concept; lower prices give you better investment opportunities.

Here is Warren Buffett on stock prices going down: "That's good for us actually, we're a net buyer of stocks over time…Just like being a net buyer of food— I expect to buy food the rest of my life and I hope that food goes down in price tomorrow. Who wouldn't rather buy at a lower price than a higher price? People are really strange on that. They should want the stock market to go down—they should want to buy at a lower price. They just feel better when stocks are going up" (qtd. in Mahomed, 2020).

However tempting it is to buy stocks while they are going up, it is always better to buy when they are going down.

Opportunity Cost

Opportunity Cost is an extremely important concept in investing. It basically means that whatever your best idea is, you should not be investing in anything worse than that. Here is a better explanation from the great Charlie Munger:

"I would argue that one filter that's useful in investing is the idea of opportunity costs. If you have one idea that is available in large quantity that is better than 98% of the other opportunities, then you can just screen out the other 98%. With this attitude you get a concentrated portfolio, which we do not mind. That practice of ours which is so simple is not widely copied, I do not know why. Even at great universities and intellectual institutions. It's an interesting question: If we're right, why are so many other places so wrong?" - Charlie Munger ("Buffett explains intrinsic value – Warren buffet on investment," 2013)

Charlie is saying that if you have a great investment and can continue to put more money into this investment, then obviously you do not need to put any money into an investment that is worse. Seems obvious? Most people do not understand this.

If the 10 yr. treasury is at 1%, then you do not have to think about an investment that you think will yield less than 1%. Same if the 10 yr. treasury were at 10%. If the 10 yr. were at 10%, you could throw out any investment that would return less than 10%. If you cannot find an investment that beats 10% there is no need to stress, just buy the 10 yr. treasury.

Your job as an investor is to print these "coupons," or the "rate of return" on the companies you are interested in. You are not going to be able to print a coupon on every company. With many companies, you may not understand their business, or you may not be able to picture it 10 years down the road, or picture how it will stand against its competitors. However, when you can understand a company, that is when you attempt to print their coupon or rate of return. There is not a precise method, but this is the job of the investor.

For example, Apple is personally my favorite company and I think I understand the business, its products, and its competitors well enough to print a coupon. We will talk more about this later, but for now I will say a conservative estimate for the "coupon" or the return on Apple would around 2.3%. I got this number by dividing their earnings by the market cap. Apple had a net income (earnings) of $55 Billion in 2019. They are currently selling for $2.4 Trillion. So simply take 55 Billion and divide it by 2.4 trillion and you will get .023 or 2.3%. I believe Apple is going to continue to increase their earnings at a small rate, but they use most of their earnings each year to pay dividends and buyback stock. Thus, I would say a 2.3% return is a conservative estimate. Anyway, this is not an incredible return which is why I am not buying it currently, but this is a lot better than the 10 yr. treasury which is 1.1%. So now your benchmark is 2.3% and you do not even think about buying a company that is going to give you a return worse than that. You just continually make these comparisons while you look for investments. Remember, if you do not understand the business, do not invest in it.

Two basic opportunities cost are the 10 yr. treasury, which is currently at 1.09%, and the S&P 500. The S&P 500 is currently selling at 38 Price-to-Earnings (PE), giving it an earnings yield of 2.6%. American businesses are going to continue to increase earnings over time at a small rate, so I would say it is safe to assume the S&P 500 is going to return 2.6%, and probably slightly better than that due to increasing earnings and the ability to buy back shares. So, when looking at any investment today you need to be extremely confident it is going to return more than 2.6%, or you can just forget about it and buy the S&P instead.

The S&P does not typically trade at these levels; the S&P's PE Ratio has only been higher twice—before the Dot com era bust and before the 2008 crash. However, interest rates today are much lower than in previous years, making it much harder to find decent investments. The median PE Ratio for the S&P is around 15. This is an earnings yield of 6.66%. At those levels you need to find investments that will for sure have a better return than 6.66%. If not just buy the S&P 500.

Financial Statements

You need to become comfortable reading a company's **financial statements**: these statements include the **Income Statement, Balance Sheet, and Statement of Cash Flows**. With all three of these statements, you need to remember companies' managers and accountants can do a lot to make them look better than they really are, so beware. If it seems sketchy it probably is.

Income Statement

The income statement is pretty straightforward as it is simply a statement of the company's income. Here is an example of my favorite company, Apple:

	2019	2018	2017	2016	2015
Revenue & Gross Profit					
Total Revenue	**260,174**	**265,595**	**229,234**	**215,639**	**233,715**
Operating Expenses					
Cost of Revenue, Total	161,782	163,756	141,048	131,376	140,089
Selling/Gen/Admin Expense	18,245	15,043	13,597	12,642	12,854
Labor & Related Expense	--	1,662	1,664	1,552	1,475
Sell/Gen/Admin Expenses, Total	18,245	16,705	15,261	14,194	14,329
Research & Development	16,217	14,236	11,581	10,045	8,067
Total Operating Expense	**196,244**	**194,697**	**167,890**	**155,615**	**162,485**
Operating Income					
Total Operating Income	**63,930**	**70,898**	**61,344**	**60,024**	**71,230**

This chart is the top section of Apple's Income statement. It simply looks at the last 5 years. The first line is revenue. Revenue is any product or service the company sold for the year. These numbers are in millions so 260,174 is $260 Billion for 2019.

Everything below revenue are operating expenses. The "cost of revenue" line represents how much the products cost to make, $161 Billion. The next line is selling/Gen/Admin expense; it includes any cost that does not have to do with production. These costs could be rent, advertising, travel, accounting, management salaries, etc. Next, research and development costs are exactly what they sound like—the company spending money to continue to create innovative and profitable products.

Operating income is the total revenue subtracted by the operating expense. In 2019, Apple's operating income was over 63 Billion dollars.

Here is the next section of the income statement, non-operating income & expenses, income taxes, extraordinary items and net income:

Non-Operating Income & Expenses					
Interest Expense, Net Non-Operating	-3,576	-3,240	-2,323	-1,456	-733
Interest Income, Non-Operating	4,961	5,686	5,201	3,999	2,921
Interest/Investment Income, Non-Operating	4,961	5,686	5,201	3,999	2,921
Other Non-Operation Income (Expense)	422	-441	-133	-1,195	-903
Other, Net	422	-441	-133	-1,195	-903
Income Before Tax	65,737	72,903	64,089	61,372	72,515
Income Taxes					
Provision for Income Taxes	10,481	11,872	15,738	15,685	19,121
Net Income After Taxes	55,256	61,031	48,351	45,687	53,394
Minority Interest & Equity in Affiliates					
Net Income Before Extra Items	55,256	61,031	48,351	45,687	53,394
Extraordinary Items					
Extraordinary Item	--	-1,500	--	--	--
Total Extraordinary Items	--	-1,500	--	--	--
Net Income					
Net Income	55,256	59,531	48,351	45,687	53,394

Non-operating income & expenses are the money paid for the interest on the loans your company has. Interest income is the exact opposite, you are recieving money for loans paid out to others. The main thing in this section is looking to see if anything looks weird. For example, if in 2019 a company had $20 Billion in non-operating income, you would want to figure out what that was, and probably not consider it true earnings.

Provision for income taxes is simply the money expected to be paid from income taxes.

The next section is extraordinary items: in 2018 Apple had an extraordinary expense of $1.5 Billion. As you can see, this was a 1-time thing and nothing to worry about. Some companies have extraordinary expenses every year. If it is every year, obviously there is nothing extraordinary about it. If a company had a giant income in extraordinary items, you would want to check it out and probably not calculate it into your valuation. After taking all those items into account, the Net Income for Apple in 2019 was $55 Billion. Which is very impressive.

Now, if we were trying to value Apple by only looking at earnings, it is much more complicated than just looking at earnings, but I will show you some thoughts here. Apple is a great company, probably the best in the world right now. It is selling for $2.4 Trillion. With $55 billion in earnings, that is a PE ratio of 43.63. Divide 100 by 43.63 and you will get only 2.3%. Or divide 55 Billion by 2.4 Trillion and get .023 or 2.3%. That is not a fantastic return on the money you are putting in. But you always want to compare this to your best idea.

As stated earlier, anyone can put money into a 10 Year Government Treasury and expect its return. The United States, like a Lannister, always pays its debts. The current 10 Yr. Treasury rate is only 1.1%. Apple is currently yielding 2.3%, so I think Apple can beat 1.1%. Thus, Apple is the superior investment. Then looking at the S&P, it is trading at 38 PE, which is an earnings yield 2.63%. I believe that Apple will be able to increase their earnings per share more than the average company in the U.S. So, I think Apple is still slightly superior to the S&P 500 at current levels. However, this is a very small margin of safety, which is why I am not currently buying any more of Apple's stock, even though it is my favorite company.

Next, you should look at other companies and think about their future and see if they can outdo Apple. Continue this process repeatedly, trying to find the best company to put your money into. If the 10 Yr. treasury were at 10%, which it has been in the past, then the treasury would likely be the much better investment. The main difference is that the government bond rate is set in stone. While companies like Apple can have earnings that fluctuate up and down, they must return that money to you in either dividends, buybacks, or retained earnings to earn more money. We will get to these later.

Continuing the Income Statement

EPS Reconciliation					
Basic/Primary Weighted Average Shares	18,471	19,822	20,869	21,883	23,014
Basic/Primary EPS Excl. Extra. Items	2.99	3.08	2.32	2.09	2.32
Basic/Primary EPS Incl. Extra. Items	2.99	3	2.32	2.09	2.32
Diluted Weighted Average Shares	18,596	20,000	21,007	22,001	23,172
Diluted EPS Excl. Extra. Items	2.97	3.05	2.3	2.08	2.3
Diluted EPS Incl. Extra. Items	2.97	2.98	2.3	2.08	2.3
Common Stock Dividends					
DPS - Common Stock Primary Issue	0.75	0.68	0.6	0.55	0.5
Gross Dividend - Common Stock	14,129	13,735	12,563	11,965	11,431

This chart shows you the company's earnings per share number and the amount of dividends they distributed. Looking at Apple's in 2019, they paid $.75/share of dividends. So, if you owned 100 shares of apple you would have received 75 dollars. Below that line is gross dividend, which is how much total cash the company gave away to shareholders, in this case over $14 Billion. Remember, these values are in millions. You will hear the term "dividend yield" and that is just the percentage of a dividend you are getting if you invested in the company today. For example, Apple paid .75 dividends per share and its stock is selling for $145; that is a dividend yield of 0.54%. (0.75 divided by 145 equals .0054, which equals .54%). Here is the rest of the income statement:

Pro Forma Net Income					
Pro Forma Net Income					
Supplemental Items					
Interest Expense, Supplemental	3,576	3,240	2,323	1,456	733
Depreciation, Supplemental	12,547	10,903	8,200	8,300	9,200
Normalized Income					
Normalized Income Before Tax	**65,737**	**72,903**	**64,089**	**61,372**	**72,515**
Income Tax Exempt Impact of Special Items	10,481	11,872	15,738	15,685	19,121
Normalized Income After Tax	55,256	61,031	48,351	45,687	53,394
Normalized Income Avail to Common	55,256	61,031	48,351	45,687	53,394
Basic Normalized EPS	2.99	3.08	2.32	2.09	2.32
Diluted Normalized EPS	2.97	3.05	2.3	2.08	2.3

Looking at the rest of this chart you just want to make sure nothing looks too out of the ordinary. This chart looks pretty good. The income matches the results above. For reference, here is the full income statement:

	2019	2018	2017	2016	2015
Revenue & Gross Profit					
Total Revenue	**260,174**	**265,595**	**229,234**	**215,639**	**233,715**
Operating Expenses					
Cost of Revenue, Total	161,782	163,756	141,048	131,376	140,089
Selling/Gen/Admin Expense	18,245	15,043	13,597	12,642	12,854
Labor & Related Expense	--	1,662	1,664	1,552	1,475
Sell/Gen/Admin Expenses, Total	18,245	16,705	15,261	14,194	14,329
Research & Development	16,217	14,236	11,581	10,045	8,067
Total Operating Expense	**196,244**	**194,697**	**167,890**	**155,615**	**162,485**
Operating Income					
Total Operating Income	**63,930**	**70,898**	**61,344**	**60,024**	**71,230**
Non-Operating Income & Expenses					
Interest Expense, Net Non-Operating	-3,576	-3,240	-2,323	-1,456	-733
Interest Income, Non-Operating	4,961	5,686	5,201	3,999	2,921
Interest/Investment Income, Non-Operating	4,961	5,686	5,201	3,999	2,921
Other Non-Operation Income (Expense)	422	-441	-133	-1,195	-903
Other, Net	422	-441	-133	-1,195	-903
Income Before Tax	**65,737**	**72,903**	**64,089**	**61,372**	**72,515**
Income Taxes					
Provision for Income Taxes	10,481	11,872	15,738	15,685	19,121
Net Income After Taxes	55,256	61,031	48,351	45,687	53,394
Minority Interest & Equity in Affiliates					
Net Income Before Extra Items	55,256	61,031	48,351	45,687	53,394
Extraordinary Items					
Extraordinary Item	--	-1,500	--	--	--
Total Extraordinary Items	--	-1,500	--	--	--
Net Income					
Net Income	**55,256**	**59,531**	**48,351**	**45,687**	**53,394**
EPS Reconciliation					
Basic/Primary Weighted Average Shares	18,471	19,822	20,869	21,883	23,014
Basic/Primary EPS Excl. Extra. Items	2.99	3.08	2.32	2.09	2.32
Basic/Primary EPS Incl. Extra. Items	2.99	3	2.32	2.09	2.32
Diluted Weighted Average Shares	18,596	20,000	21,007	22,001	23,172
Diluted EPS Excl. Extra. Items	2.97	3.05	2.3	2.08	2.3
Diluted EPS Incl. Extra. Items	2.97	2.98	2.3	2.08	2.3
Common Stock Dividends					
DPS - Common Stock Primary Issue	0.75	0.68	0.6	0.55	0.5
Gross Dividend - Common Stock	14,129	13,735	12,563	11,965	11,431
Pro Forma Net Income					
Pro Forma Net Income					
Supplemental Items					
Interest Expense, Supplemental	3,576	3,240	2,323	1,456	733
Depreciation, Supplemental	12,547	10,903	8,200	8,300	9,200
Normalized Income					
Normalized Income Before Tax	**65,737**	**72,903**	**64,089**	**61,372**	**72,515**
Income Tax Exempt Impact of Special Items	10,481	11,872	15,738	15,685	19,121
Normalized Income After Tax	55,256	61,031	48,351	45,687	53,394
Normalized Income Avail to Common	55,256	61,031	48,351	45,687	53,394
Basic Normalized EPS	2.99	3.08	2.32	2.09	2.32
Diluted Normalized EPS	2.97	3.05	2.3	2.08	2.3

Balance Sheet

The balance sheet is basically the health of your company. You want a balance sheet with little debt compared to assets and income. If your company has more debt than assets and the company makes little or no money, then that is a recipe for death—aka bankruptcy. If your company goes bankrupt your stock goes to 0. Anything times 0 is 0. Obviously, you do not want to put your hard-earned money into a company that goes to 0. I lost about 25% of all net worth in a company that went to 0.

Here is Apple's balance sheet. We will start off with the current assets.

	2019	2018	2017	2016	2015
Assets					
Cash	12,204	11,575	7,982	8,601	11,389
Cash & Equivalents	36,640	14,338	12,307	11,883	9,731
Short Term Investments	51,713	40,388	53,892	46,671	20,481
Cash and Short Term Investments	100,557	66,301	74,181	67,155	41,601
Trade Accounts Receivable, Gross	--	--	--	15,807	16,912
Provision for Doubtful Accounts	--	--	--	-53	-63
Trade Accounts Receivable, Net	22,926	23,186	17,874	15,754	16,849
Other Receivables	22,878	25,809	17,799	13,545	13,494
Total Receivables, Net	45,804	48,995	35,673	29,299	30,343
Total Inventory	4,106	3,956	4,855	2,132	2,349
Restricted Cash - Current	23	--	--	--	--
Other Current Assets	12,329	12,087	13,936	8,283	15,085
Other Current Assets, Total	12,352	12,087	13,936	8,283	15,085
Total Current Assets	162,819	131,339	128,645	106,869	89,378

Current assets are supposed to be assets that can be quickly converted to cash. But with most companies a lot of assets are good until reached for, meaning they look good on paper, but you cannot get them. The management and accountants can make something look good on paper but when the company actually needs the assets they are no where to be found. So, whatever you see in the balance sheet and all other reports, just know that managers and accountants can make them look a lot better than they are. Eventually the truth will come out.

Looking at Apple's balance sheet we see they have over $12 Billion in the "cash" line, and over $100 Billion in the "cash and short-term investments" line. That is very good. You want companies with a healthy amount of cash. Total Receivables is how much your costumers owe you for goods or services. Total Inventory is how many goods the company has that have not been sold. Other current assets can be examined in the annual report. These assets are not as reliable as a figure like cash:

Buildings	10,283	9,075	8,205	7,279	6,517
Land/Improvements	17,952	17,085	16,216	13,587	10,185
Machinery/Equipment	75,291	69,797	65,982	54,210	44,543
Other Property/Plant/Equipment	8,570	--	--	--	--
Property/Plant/Equipment - Gross	112,096	95,957	90,403	75,076	61,245
Accumulated Depreciation	-66,760	-58,579	-49,099	-41,293	-34,235
Property/Plant/Equipment - Net	45,336	37,378	41,304	33,783	27,010
Goodwill, Net	--	--	--	--	5,414
Intangibles, Gross	--	--	--	--	9,012
Accumulated Intangible Amortization	--	--	--	--	-5,806
Intangibles, Net	--	--	--	--	3,206
Long Term Investments - Other	100,887	105,341	170,799	194,714	170,430
Long Term Investments	100,887	105,341	170,799	194,714	170,430
Restricted Cash - Long Term	1,737	1,357	--	--	--
Other Long Term Assets	32,215	31,621	22,283	18,177	8,757
Total Assets	323,888	338,516	365,725	375,319	321,686

Here are the long-term assets of Apple. As you can see, these assets include Buildings, Land, Equipment,

Property, and Investments. Two categories that are important to look at are **goodwill** and **intangibles**. These are considered intangible assets. Apple does not have any of these values. When I go through a Balance sheet, I simply subtract those as Assets because it is extremely hard to value those assets. By subtracting goodwill and intangibles this gives us the company's *tangible* assets. Again, accountants can make those numbers look a lot better than they are.

Now, let's take a look at Apple's liabilities:

Liabilities					
Accounts Payable	42,296	46,236	55,888	44,242	37,294
Accrued Expenses	1,436	--	--	--	20,951
Notes Payable/Short Term Debt	4,996	5,980	11,964	11,977	8,105
Current Portion of Long-Term Debt/Capital Liabilities	8,797	10,260	8,784	6,496	3,500
Customer Advances	6,643	5,522	5,966	7,548	8,080
Other Current Liabilities	41,224	37,720	33,327	30,551	1,076
Other Current Liabilities, Total	47,867	43,242	39,293	38,099	9,156
Total Current Liabilities	105,392	105,718	115,929	100,814	79,006
Capital Lease Obligations	637	--	--	--	--
Total Long Term Debt	99,304	91,807	93,735	97,207	75,427
Total Debt	113,097	108,047	114,483	115,680	87,032
Deferred Income Tax	--	--	--	31,504	26,019
Other Liabilities, Total	53,853	50,503	48,914	11,747	12,985
Total Liabilities	258,549	248,028	258,578	241,272	193,437

Current Liabilities are liabilities or debts due within 12 months. Simply put, you want your company to have more current assets than liabilities. Apple has over $162 Billion in current assets and over $100 Billion in Cash and short-term investments, with only $105 Billion in current Liabilities. This is a conservative balance sheet for a tech company. The remaining liabilities are considered long-term liabilities and are due later than 1 year.

Overall, Apple has $323 Billion in Total Assets and $258 Billion in Total Liabilities. **You do not want a company with more liabilities than assets unless they earn a high rate of income**.

The next part of the balance sheet is Stockholder Equity:

Shareholder Equity					
Common Stock	50,779	45,174	40,201	35,867	31,251
Retained Earnings (Accumulated Deficit)	14,966	45,898	70,400	98,330	96,364
Unrealized Gain (Loss)	1,846	707	-3,209	328	1,174
Cumulative Translation Adjustment	-1,375	-1,463	-1,055	-354	-578
Other Comprehensive Income	-877	172	810	-124	38
Other Equity, Total	-2,252	-1,291	-245	-478	-540
Total Equity	65,339	90,488	107,147	134,047	128,249
Total Liabilities & Shareholders' Equity	323,888	338,516	365,725	375,319	321,686
Total Common Shares Outstanding	16,977	17,773	19,020	20,505	21,345
Treasury Shares-Common Primary Issue	0	0	0	0	0

Stockholders' Equity is the Total Assets minus Total Liabilities. Subtract Apple's $323 Billion by $258 Billion, and you will get $65 Billion for stockholders' Equity. An important item to examine is the Total Common Shares Outstanding. As you can see, Apple's has gone down every year for the last 5 years. This is good for the owner because it means you own more of the company. If the company is giving away shares, then they better be making a lot more money in order to keep the EPS (Earnings Per share) going up. Otherwise, they are giving your company away. Companies in desperate need for cash will issue shares to pay off current debts.

Below is the entire Balance sheet:

	2019	2018	2017	2016	2015
Assets					
Cash	12,204	11,575	7,982	8,601	11,389
Cash & Equivalents	36,640	14,338	12,307	11,883	9,731
Short Term Investments	51,713	40,388	53,892	46,671	20,481
Cash and Short Term Investments	100,557	66,301	74,181	67,155	41,601
Trade Accounts Receivable, Gross	--	--	--	15,807	16,912
Provision for Doubtful Accounts	--	--	--	-53	-63
Trade Accounts Receivable, Net	22,926	23,186	17,874	15,754	16,849
Other Receivables	22,878	25,809	17,799	13,545	13,494
Total Receivables, Net	45,804	48,995	35,673	29,299	30,343
Total Inventory	4,106	3,956	4,855	2,132	2,349
Restricted Cash - Current	23	--	--	--	--
Other Current Assets	12,329	12,087	13,936	8,283	15,085
Other Current Assets, Total	12,352	12,087	13,936	8,283	15,085
Total Current Assets	162,819	131,339	128,645	106,869	89,378
Buildings	10,283	9,075	8,205	7,279	6,517
Land/Improvements	17,952	17,085	16,216	13,587	10,185
Machinery/Equipment	75,291	69,797	65,982	54,210	44,543
Other Property/Plant/Equipment	8,570	--	--	--	--
Property/Plant/Equipment - Gross	112,096	95,957	90,403	75,076	61,245
Accumulated Depreciation	-66,760	-58,579	-49,099	-41,293	-34,235
Property/Plant/Equipment - Net	45,336	37,378	41,304	33,783	27,010
Goodwill, Net	--	--	--	--	5,414
Intangibles, Gross	--	--	--	--	9,012
Accumulated Intangible Amortization	--	--	--	--	-5,806
Intangibles, Net	--	--	--	--	3,206
Long Term Investments - Other	100,887	105,341	170,799	194,714	170,430
Long Term Investments	100,887	105,341	170,799	194,714	170,430
Restricted Cash - Long Term	1,737	1,357	--	--	--
Other Long Term Assets	32,215	31,621	22,283	18,177	8,757
Total Assets	323,888	338,516	365,725	375,319	321,686
Liabilities					
Accounts Payable	42,296	46,236	55,888	44,242	37,294
Accrued Expenses	1,436	--	--	--	20,951
Notes Payable/Short Term Debt	4,996	5,980	11,964	11,977	8,105
Current Portion of Long-Term Debt/Capital Lial	8,797	10,260	8,784	6,496	3,500
Customer Advances	6,643	5,522	5,966	7,548	8,080
Other Current Liabilities	41,224	37,720	33,327	30,551	1,076
Other Current Liabilities, Total	47,867	43,242	39,293	38,099	9,156
Total Current Liabilities	105,392	105,718	115,929	100,814	79,006
Capital Lease Obligations	637	--	--	--	--
Total Long Term Debt	99,304	91,807	93,735	97,207	75,427
Total Debt	113,097	108,047	114,483	115,680	87,032
Deferred Income Tax	--	--	--	31,504	26,019
Other Liabilities, Total	53,853	50,503	48,914	11,747	12,985
Total Liabilities	258,549	248,028	258,578	241,272	193,437
Shareholder Equity					
Common Stock	50,779	45,174	40,201	35,867	31,251
Retained Earnings (Accumulated Deficit)	14,966	45,898	70,400	98,330	96,364
Unrealized Gain (Loss)	1,846	707	-3,209	328	1,174
Cumulative Translation Adjustment	-1,375	-1,463	-1,055	-354	-578
Other Comprehensive Income	-877	172	810	-124	38
Other Equity, Total	-2,252	-1,291	-245	-478	-540
Total Equity	65,339	90,488	107,147	134,047	128,249
Total Liabilities & Shareholders' Equity	323,888	338,516	365,725	375,319	321,686
Total Common Shares Outstanding	16,977	17,773	19,020	20,505	21,345
Treasury Shares-Common Primary Issue	0	0	0	0	0

Statement of Cash Flows

Cash Flows are the most advanced and complicated of Statements, as they require the most thinking. To begin, here is Apple's Cash from Operating Activities:

	2019	2018	2017	2016	2015
Cash From Operating Activities					
Net Income	57,411	55,256	59,531	48,351	45,687
Depreciation/Depletion	11,056	12,547	10,903	10,157	10,505
Deferred Taxes	-215	-340	-32,590	5,966	4,938
Other Non-Cash Items	6,732	5,416	4,896	4,674	4,696
Non-Cash Items	6,732	5,416	4,896	4,674	4,696
Cash Taxes Paid, Supplemental	9,501	15,263	10,417	11,591	10,444
Cash Interest Paid, Supplemental	3,002	3,423	3,022	2,092	1,316
Accounts Receivable	8,470	3,176	-13,332	-6,347	476
Inventories	-127	-289	828	-2,723	217
Other Assets	-9,588	873	-423	-5,318	1,055
Accounts Payable	-4,062	-1,923	9,175	8,966	2,117
Changes in Working Capital	5,690	-3,488	34,694	-4,923	405
Total Cash from Operations	80,674	69,391	77,434	64,225	66,231

While the above chart may seem complicated, there is one important thing that we can quickly observe in the final line: Total Cash from Operations. Apple's total cash from operation is positive. Keep in mind, **if the Total Cash from Operations is negative, that is a huge red flag.**

In the next chart, we can see Apple's Cash From Investing Activities:

Cash From Investing Activities					
Capital Expenditures	-7,309	-10,495	-13,313	-12,451	-12,734
Acquisition of Business	-1,524	-624	-721	-329	-297
Sale/Maturity of Investment	120,483	98,724	104,072	126,465	111,794
Purchase of Investments	-115,148	-40,631	-73,227	-160,007	-143,816
Other Investing Cash Flow	-791	-1,078	-745	-124	-924
Other Investment Cash Flow Items, Total	3,020	56,391	29,379	-33,995	-33,243
Total Cash from Investing	-4,289	45,896	16,066	-46,446	-45,977

When looking at a company's Cash from Investing Activities, you want to look at the Capital Expenditures. If the capital expenditures are above or even close to the net income of the business, this likely means that you are in a difficult business. Think of airlines; pretty much all profit must be used just to remain as competitive as you were last year. In the above chart, Apple's capital expenditures were $7 Billion, compared to $57 Billion in Net Income. This is a good ratio.

Here is Charlie Munger's take on 2 different kinds of business:

> "There are two kinds of businesses: The first earns twelve percent, and you can take the profits out at the end of the year. The second earns twelve percent, but all the excess cash must be reinvested— there is never any cash. It reminds me of the guy who sells construction equipment— he looks at his used machines, taken in as customers bought new ones, and says, 'There's all of my profit, rusting in my yard.' We hate that kind of business." – Charlie Munger (qtd. in Haque, 2020).

The second business is the kind where the capital expenditures are equal to the net income.

In the next chart, we can see Apple's Cash from Financing Activities:

Cash From Financing Activities					
Financing Cash Flow Items	-3,760	-2,922	-2,527	-1,874	-1,570
Total Cash Dividends Paid	-14,081	-14,119	-13,712	-12,769	-12,150
Sale/Issuance of Common	880	781	669	555	495
Repurchase/Retirement Common	-72,358	-66,897	-72,738	-32,900	-29,722
Common Stock, Net	-71,478	-66,116	-72,069	-32,345	-29,227
Issuance (Retirement) of Stock, Net	-71,478	-66,116	-72,069	-32,345	-29,227
Short Term Debt, Net	-963	-5,977	-37	3,852	-397
Long Term Debt, Net	16,091	6,963	6,969	28,662	24,954
Total Debt Reduction	-12,629	-8,805	-6,500	-3,500	-2,500
Issue (Retirement) of Debt, Net	2,499	-7,819	432	29,014	22,057
Total Cash from Financing	-86,820	-90,976	-87,876	-17,974	-20,890

When looking at a company, I like looking at financing activities the best because they show you how much money investors are getting back through dividends and buying back shares. The Total Cash dividends paid was $14 Billion. Compare the Total Cash to how much the company is selling in order to figure out what dividend yield you are receiving. If Apple is selling for $2.4 Trillion, divide 14 Billion by 2.4 trillion and get .0058, or .58%. So, if you invested 100 dollars in Apple today you would receive 58 cents back after a year of dividends. That is not a lot of money. However, what I think is more important is stock buy backs. Apple bought back $71 Billion of stock last year. At $2.4 Trillion, Apple bought back about 2.9% of stock in 2019 (71 Billion divided by 2.4 Trillion). These numbers do not sound like a lot, but over time you will continue to own more and more of the company.

The next Statement is Net Change in Cash. Here is Apple's Net Change in Cash:

Net Change in Cash	-10,435	24,311	5,624	-195	-636
Net Cash - Begin Balance/Reserved for Future Use	50,224	25,913	20,289	20,484	21,120
Net Cash - End Balance/Reserved for Future Use	39,789	50,224	25,913	20,289	20,484
Depreciation, Supplemental	11,056	12,547	10,903	10,157	10,505
Cash Interest Paid, Supplemental	3,002	3,423	3,022	2,092	1,316
Cash Taxes Paid, Supplemental	9,501	15,263	10,417	11,591	10,444

The net change in cash adds each of the three different sections. In 2019, Apple's Net Cash went down by $10.4 Billion, which would be concerning if they had not given back $85 Billion to shareholders, $14 Billion in dividends, and $71 Billion in buying back stock.

Below is the entire statement of Cash Flows:

	2019	2018	2017	2016	2015
Cash From Operating Activities					
Net Income	57,411	55,256	59,531	48,351	45,687
Depreciation/Depletion	11,056	12,547	10,903	10,157	10,505
Deferred Taxes	-215	-340	-32,590	5,966	4,938
Other Non-Cash Items	6,732	5,416	4,896	4,674	4,696
Non-Cash Items	6,732	5,416	4,896	4,674	4,696
Cash Taxes Paid, Supplemental	9,501	15,263	10,417	11,591	10,444
Cash Interest Paid, Supplemental	3,002	3,423	3,022	2,092	1,316
Accounts Receivable	8,470	3,176	-13,332	-6,347	476
Inventories	-127	-289	828	-2,723	217
Other Assets	-9,588	873	-423	-5,318	1,055
Accounts Payable	-4,062	-1,923	9,175	8,966	2,117
Changes in Working Capital	5,690	-3,488	34,694	-4,923	405
Total Cash from Operations	80,674	69,391	77,434	64,225	66,231
Cash From Investing Activities					
Capital Expenditures	-7,309	-10,495	-13,313	-12,451	-12,734
Acquisition of Business	-1,524	-624	-721	-329	-297
Sale/Maturity of Investment	120,483	98,724	104,072	126,465	111,794
Purchase of Investments	-115,148	-40,631	-73,227	-160,007	-143,816
Other Investing Cash Flow	-791	-1,078	-745	-124	-924
Other Investment Cash Flow Items, Total	3,020	56,391	29,379	-33,995	-33,243
Total Cash from Investing	-4,289	45,896	16,066	-46,446	-45,977
Cash From Financing Activities					
Financing Cash Flow Items	-3,760	-2,922	-2,527	-1,874	-1,570
Total Cash Dividends Paid	-14,081	-14,119	-13,712	-12,769	-12,150
Sale/Issuance of Common	880	781	669	555	495
Repurchase/Retirement Common	-72,358	-66,897	-72,738	-32,900	-29,722
Common Stock, Net	-71,478	-66,116	-72,069	-32,345	-29,227
Issuance (Retirement) of Stock, Net	-71,478	-66,116	-72,069	-32,345	-29,227
Short Term Debt, Net	-963	-5,977	-37	3,852	-397
Long Term Debt, Net	16,091	6,963	6,969	28,662	24,954
Total Debt Reduction	-12,629	-8,805	-6,500	-3,500	-2,500
Issue (Retirement) of Debt, Net	2,499	-7,819	432	29,014	22,057
Total Cash from Financing	-86,820	-90,976	-87,876	-17,974	-20,890
Net Change in Cash	-10,435	24,311	5,624	-195	-636
Net Cash - Begin Balance/Reserved for Future Use	50,224	25,913	20,289	20,484	21,120
Net Cash - End Balance/Reserved for Future Use	39,789	50,224	25,913	20,289	20,484
Depreciation, Supplemental	11,056	12,547	10,903	10,157	10,505
Cash Interest Paid, Supplemental	3,002	3,423	3,022	2,092	1,316
Cash Taxes Paid, Supplemental	9,501	15,263	10,417	11,591	10,444

Apple's financial reports taken from Charles Schwabs Website. (Charles Schwab | A modern approach to investing & retirement, n.d.)

The main thing you need to remember for investing is you are not buying a symbol that moves up and down, you are buying a business. No matter how good the business is, there is a price that is too expensive to pay for it. This price has nothing to do with the stock price; it is the **market cap**. A $1.00 per share company can be overpriced and a $360,000 per share company can be underpriced. When you are buying stock, **you want stock prices to go down not up,** so you can buy the same company for less. Next, we will talk about my **VERY** stupid mistakes.

Section 3: Pre-Intelligent Investor

This section I will go over the stupid mistakes I made before having a clue what I was doing, I was just listening to what "experts" were telling me online. I will simply go over some of the stupid investments I made before I read *The Intelligent Investor*.

S&P 500

The first investment I made was a Charles Schwab Index fund that mirrors the S&P 500. I bought it my Senior year of high school on 3/31/2014. At that time, the S&P 500 was at $1,873. My mistake was not in buying the S&P, it was selling. I sold all my S&P 500 by 4/19/2016. On that date I sold it at $2,100. After 2 years, I had accumulated a modest gain of 10.8%, or about 5.26% compounded average growth rate (CAGR). Dividends for each year were about 2%, so the real gains were more like 14.8% and about 7.26% CAGR.

If I had just left it all in there it would have saved me a lot of time, effort, frustration, and most importantly money. On the other hand, I have learned valuable lessons from my costly mistakes. On 12/13/2020 the S&P 500 was at $3,663. Over 6 years, this would have been over a 95% gain or 11.83% CAGR before dividends. After dividends, it would have been about a 107% gain and 13.83% CAGR— or perhaps a little less than this, as in 2017, 2019, and 2020, dividends were slightly less than 2%. A 13% CAGR is extremely satisfactory. A $10,000 investment at an average of 13% would be a million dollars in just 38 years, and a billion dollars in just 95 years.

For the last 100 years, the S&P 500 average return is about 10%. So, I think it is okay to expect lower returns than 13% in the future. The S&P 500 PE ratio is about 38, which means its earnings yield is only 2.6%. In 2014 when I first bought it, the S&P 500 was trading at around 19 PE, which is a 5.26% earnings yield. Back in 2014, the S&P was more attractive. However, with interest rates so low (the 10 yr. treasury rate today is 1%), the S&P 500 is still a much better investment compared to the treasury yield.

AAPL

The first individual stock I bought was Apple; this was a great investment. I knew it was good but back then I did not realize how good. I first bought Apple on 07/09/2015 for $30.88 a share, it was selling for $123.55 a share but it split 1 for 4 in 2020 so for simplicity I will refer to the price adjusted for the stock split. Remember, a stock splitting means nothing to the company, so it is irrelevant here.

My mistake in this company is simple, I did not buy enough of Apple and I sold it too soon. We still own Apple, however over the years I have bought and sold it continuously. With all the buying and selling, including dividends, I am up around 120% over a 5-year period. This amounts to about 17% CAGR. 17% CAGR is an excellent return! However, If I had simply bought Apple and held onto it, I would be up 304 %. That's a CAGR of 32%, plus another 1.5ish% with dividends. A $10,000 dollar investment with a 33% CAGR will be 1 million dollars in only 17 years, and a billion dollars in only 42 years. This is easily the biggest mistake of my career, because I knew it was a great company. However, at that point I had not read *The Intelligent Investor* or listened to Warren Buffett and Charlie Munger. Thus, I did not truly know how good of an investment it was. I will explain more about Apple in the next section.

LNCO

LNCO was the second stock I bought and it is the first bad company I bought. I lost all my investment, about 25% of my net worth in less than a year. The company went completely bankrupt and it is easy to tell why. Below is the Balance Sheet and Income Statement for 2014 and 2015.

(All values are in thousands except for unit amounts)

Balance Sheet

	2015		2014
Assets:			
Current Assets:			
Cash and cash equivalents	$2,168.00		$1,809.00
Accounts receivable – trade, net	$216,556.00		$471,684.00
Derivative instruments	$1,220,230.00		$1,077,142.00
Other current assets	$119,921.00		$155,955.00
Total current assets	$1,558,875.00		$1,706,590.00
Noncurrent assets:			
Oil and natural gas properties (successful efforts method)	$18,121,155.00		$18,068,900.00
Less accumulated depletion and amortization	(11,097,492)		(4,867,682)
	$7,023,663.00		$13,201,218.00
Other property and equipment	$708,711.00		$669,149.00
Less accumulated depreciation	(195,661)		(144,282)
	$513,050.00		$524,867.00
Derivative instruments	$566,401.00		$848,097.00
Restricted cash	$257,363.00		$6,225.00
Other noncurrent assets	$57,594.00		$136,512.00
	$881,358.00		$990,834.00
Total noncurrent assets	$8,418,071.00		$14,716,919.00
Total assets	$9,976,946.00		$16,423,509.00
LIABILITIES AND UNITHOLDERS' CAPITAL (DEFICIT)			
Current liabilities:			
Accounts payable and accrued expenses	$455,374.00		$814,809.00
Derivative instruments	$2,241.00		—
Current portion of long-term debt	$3,716,508.00		—
Other accrued liabilities	$119,593.00		$167,736.00
Total current liabilities	$4,293,716.00		$982,545.00
Noncurrent liabilities:			
Derivative instruments	$857.00		$684.00
Long-term debt, net	$5,328,235.00		$10,295,809.00
Other noncurrent liabilities	$623,039.00		$600,866.00
Total noncurrent liabilities	$5,952,131.00		$10,897,359.00
Commitments and contingencies (Note 11)			
Unitholders' capital (deficit):			
355,017,428 units and 331,974,913 units issued and outstanding at December 31, 2015, and December 31, 2014, respectively	$5,343,116.00		$5,395,811.00
Accumulated deficit	(5,612,017)		(852,206)
	(268,901)		$4,543,605.00
Total liabilities and unitholders' capital (deficit)	$9,976,946.00		$16,423,509.00

There are major red flags in this balance sheet. One major red flag is the **derivative instruments**. They have two different derivative instruments assets, one in the current assets and one in the long-term assets. The total comes to $1.8 Billion. Looking at this now, I would simply erase these values from the assets. Derivatives are very complicated, and most companies are going to overvalue these assets. Sometimes they attempt honestly, many times they do not. In general, I would say it is safer to estimate that derivative instruments are valueless.

LNCO's major asset is oil and natural gas properties, worth about $7 Billion. Again, I would be very skeptical of this value unless you trusted the company's management completely.

Doing a quick calculation for book value, you will get 9.9 Billion subtracted by 10.2 Billion (4.3 Billion current liabilities plus 5.9 non-current liabilities). You will have a book value of negative $.3 Billion or -$300 Million. If I were doing this quick calculation now, I would have subtracted $1.8 Billion for derivatives. I would also subtract about half of the $7 Billion in natural gas properties assets, leaving me with $3.5 Billion. So, my personal quick valuation shows LNCO with a value of negative $5.6 Billion (5.6 Billion). In general, this is not going to be a company you want to invest in. Only consider investing if they are making a lot of money each year consistently and you love the products and management. LNCO is not one of those cases.

If you look at the bottom of the balance sheet there are about 343 Million units. In the beginning of 2015 this company was selling for about 11 dollars a share, meaning that the entire company was selling for about $3.7 Billion (11 dollars per share multiplied by 343 Million units). It is obvious to tell that this company is not worth anything near 3.7 Billion dollars. Believe it or not online articles and "experts" were telling people to buy this company. I was one of the idiots who listened. By the end of the year, it was selling for about $1.00, and soon it was bankrupt. My entire investment was wiped out because I trusted "experts". DO NOT INVEST IN COMPANIES LIKE THESE. Here is an article in 2013 promoting this company: https://www.fool.com/investing/general/2013/10/08/3-reasons-to-buy-linn-energy.aspx (DiLallo, 2013). If you think the balance sheet was bad, LNCO's income statement is much worse. Look below:

Income Statement

	2015		2014		2013
Revenues and other:					
Oil, natural gas and natural gas liquids sales	1,726,271		3,610,539		2,073,240
Gains on oil and natural gas derivatives	1,056,189		1,206,179		177,857
Marketing revenues	74,129		135,260		54,171
Other revenues	26,745		31,325		26,387
	2,883,334		4,983,303		2,331,655
Expenses:					
Lease operating expenses	617,764		805,164		372,523
Transportation expenses	219,721		207,331		128,440
Marketing expenses	57,144		117,465		37,892
General and administrative expenses	296,887		293,073		236,271
Exploration costs	9,473		125,037		5,251
Depreciation, depletion and amortization	805,757		1,073,902		829,311
Impairment of long-lived assets	5,813,954		2,303,749		828,317
Taxes, other than income taxes	181,895		267,403		138,631
(Gains) losses on sale of assets and other, net	(197,409)		(366,500)		13,637
	7,805,186		4,826,624		2,590,273
Other income and (expenses):					
Interest expense, net of amounts capitalized	(546,453)		(587,838)		(421,137)
Gain (loss) on extinguishment of debt	719,259		—		(5,304)
Other, net	(17,226)		(16,213)		(8,477)
	155,580.00		(604,051)		(434,918)
Loss before income taxes	(4,766,272)		(447,372)		(693,536)
Net loss	(4,759,811)		(451,809)		(691,337)
Net loss per unit:					
Basic	(13.87)		(1.40)		(2.94)
Diluted	(13.87)		(1.40)		(2.94)
Weighted average units outstanding:					
Basic	343,323		328,918		237,544
Diluted	343,323		328,918		237,544
Distributions declared per unit	$0.938		$2.90		$2.90

Financial Statements from (U.S Securities and Exchange Commission, n.d.)

In the three years of 2013, 2014, and 2015, LNCO lost $690 Million, $450 Million, then a whopping $4.7 Billion dollars. This is a recipe for bankruptcy. Another thing to watch is the amount of shares a company has. In just 3 years the company's number of units went from 237 Million to 343 Million. This means that if you had money in this company in 2013, by the end of 2015 the company had given away about half your ownership in the company. This is a major red flag.

It seems obvious not to invest in a company losing so much money, but many day traders do this every day. People online told me to buy this company. I hope by the end of this book you do not even think about investing in a company like this.

DO NOT INVEST IN A COMPANY LIKE THIS!

PPCB

Here is another company where I have lost over 99% percent of my investment; PPCB has not gone bankrupt, but through dilution (a fancy word for a company issuing shares) I have lost over 99% of my investment. This investment is even easier to see why it is so bad. Again, online "experts" were saying to buy this company. PPCB is a very small drug company; they were supposed to be coming out with a cancer drug…Well, it has been 5 years and there has not been much progress on the drug.

In 2015 PPCB had $627,000 in assets, while having $3.7 Million in liabilities. So, a quick book value would tell you this company is worth about -3.1 Million dollars. Not only that, but this company has also never had 1 penny of revenue. In 2014, they lost about $830,000, and in 2015 they lost over $3.4 Million. Again, a major red flag is the company went from 72 million shares to 177 Million a year later, almost a 150% increase. **Do not invest in companies with a negative book value that have never made a sale.** I know it sounds obvious, but people convinced me to do it, and I was ignorant enough to invest in it. Check out the income statement and balance sheet below. This is how you lose your entire investment. **DO NOT INVEST IN A COMPANY LIKE THIS:**

Income Statement

	2015		2014
REVENUE			
Revenue	-		-
OPERATING EXPENSES			
Administration expenses	1,567,549		742,037
Occupancy expenses	3,719		11,016
Research and development	134,319		8,168
TOTAL OPERATING EXPENSES	1,705,587		761,221
LOSS FROM OPERATIONS	(1,705,587)		(761,221)
OTHER INCOME (EXPENSE)			
Interest expense	(1,323,902)		(93,147)
Interest income	33		18
Other expense	(50,002)		-
Change in fair value of derivative liabilities	(541,981)		(16,522)
Gain on debt settlements, net	375,547		-
Foreign currency transaction loss	(244,332)		(6,959)
TOTAL OTHER INCOME (EXPENSE)	(1,784,637)		(116,610)
LOSS BEFORE INCOME TAXES	(3,490,224)		(877,831)
INCOME TAX BENEFIT	77,470		48,267
NET LOSS	(3,412,754)		(829,564)
OTHER COMPREHENSIVE INCOME (LOSS)			
Foreign currency translation gain (loss)	403,831		(58,274)
TOTAL OTHER COMPREHENSIVE INCOME (LOSS)	(3,008,923)		(887,838)
BASIC AND DILUTED NET LOSS PER SHARE	-0.02		-0.01
BASIC AND DILUTED WEIGHTED AVERAGE SHARES OUTSTANDING	177,633,496		72,350,555

Balance Sheet

	2015	2014
ASSETS		
CURRENT ASSETS:		
Cash	107,627	87,799
GST tax receivable	11,647	946
Prepaid expenses and other current assets	502,616	25,000
TOTAL CURRENT ASSETS	621,890	113,745
Security deposit	1,684	-
Property and equipment, net	3,494	-
TOTAL ASSETS	627,068	113,745
LIABILITIES AND STOCKHOLDERS' DEFICIT		
CURRENT LIABILITIES:		
Accounts payable	236,466	350,004
Accrued expenses and other payables	386,311	422,326
Convertible notes and related accrued interest, net	1,794,375	272,424
Loans and notes payable	27,558	33,909
Embedded conversion option liabilities	780,281	-
Warrant derivative liability	269,648	158,244
Due to directors - related parties	35,108	60,350
Loans from directors and officer - related parties	79,416	161,975
Employee benefit liability	71,421	62,827
TOTAL CURRENT LIABILITIES	3,680,584	1,522,059
Commitments and Contingencies		
(See Note 9)		
STOCKHOLDERS' DEFICIT:		
Series A preferred stock, $0.01 par value; 10,000,000 shares authorized; 500,000 and 0 shares issued and outstanding as of June 30, 2015 and June 30, 2014, respectively	5,000	-
Series B preferred stock, $0.01 par value; 5 shares authorized; 1 and 0 shares issued and outstanding as of June 30, 2015 and June 30, 2014, respectively	-	-
Common stock, $0.001 par value; 2,000,000,000 shares authorized; 347,442,013 and 72,684,767 shares issued and outstanding as of June 30, 2015 and June 30, 2014, respectively	347,442	72,685
Additional paid-in capital	17,458,745	16,374,781
Accumulated other comprehensive income (loss)	100,968	(302,863)
Accumulated deficit	(20,965,671)	(17,552,917)
TOTAL STOCKHOLDERS' DEFICIT	(3,053,516)	(1,408,314)
TOTAL LIABILITIES AND STOCKHOLDERS' DEFICIT	627,068	113,745

Statements from (United States Securities and Exchange Commission, n.d.)

SPYR

SPYR was another horrible investment, but it does not look quite as bad when looking at the income statement and balance sheet. That is why investing is a lot more than just looking at statements; you must think and read to be an investor. Even though SPYR might look better, I still lost 80 percent of my investment in this company. The worst part of this stock was it gave me false confidence in my stock picking. After about a month of owning this company, it had gone up 100% and I sold my profits. I eventually bought back in and lost over 80% of my investment. That was a stupid mistake.

I bought SPYR in 2015. That year the company had over 150 million shares outstanding and the highest it traded for was 99 cents, meaning the company was selling for about $150 Million (aka market cap 150 Million). Let us look at the **Balance Sheet**:

Balance Sheet

ASSETS	2015		2014
Current Assets:			
Cash and cash equivalents	6,903,887		6,994,180
Accounts receivable, net	7,701		4,271
Inventory	12,957		14,499
Prepaid expenses	55,533		60,819
Capitalized licensing rights	80,000		—
Trading securities, at market value	324,444		6,026,780
Total Current Assets	7,384,522		13,100,549
Property and equipment, net	274,886		155,250
Intangible assets, net	21,307		5,000
Other assets	22,299		15,000
TOTAL ASSETS	7,703,014		13,275,799
LIABILITIES AND STOCKHOLDERS' EQUITY			
LIABILITIES			
Current Liabilities:			
Accounts payable and accrued liabilities	104,871		72,550
Related party accounts payable	7,506		270,000
Total Current Liabilities	112,377		342,550
COMMITMENTS AND CONTINGENCIES			
STOCKHOLDERS' EQUITY			
Preferred stock, $0.0001 par value, 10,000,000 shares authorized			
107,636 Class A shares issued and outstanding as of December 31, 2015 and 2014	11		11
20,000 Class E shares issued and outstanding as of December 31, 2015 and 2014	2		2
Common Stock, $0.0001 par value, 250,000,000 shares authorized			
151,508,127 and 140,627,710 shares issued and outstanding as of December 31, 2015 and December 31, 2014	15,151		14,063
Common stock issuable, 0 and 5,500,000 shares as of December 31, 2015 and December 31, 2014	—		987,500
Additional paid-in capital	31,269,822		26,681,601
Accumulated deficit	(23,694,349)		(14,749,928)
Total Stockholders' Equity	7,590,637		12,933,249
TOTAL LIABILITIES AND STOCKHOLDERS' EQUITY	7,703,014		13,275,799

In the chart above, SPYR balance shows about $7.7 Million in assets with about $6.9 million coming from cash, with only $112 thousand in liabilities. This is a good-looking balance sheet in terms of not going bankrupt. So, we give it a quick book value of around $7.6 Million. However, I said above that SPYR was selling for $150 Million (Market Cap 150 Million). This price equals a Price to Book (PB) Ratio of 19.7 (150 Million divided by 7.6 Million equals 19.73). That ratio indicates a huge premium on book value. If you are going to buy a company that is selling for this much over book value, you would want very consistent earnings and earnings that are going to be returned to shareholders. Now that our suspicions have been raised, we must look at the **Income Statement**:

Income Statement

	2015			2014
Revenues	1,596,812			1,450,887
Cost of sales	472,986			510,089
Gross Margin	1,123,826			940,798
Expenses				
Labor and related expenses	1,718,636			332,669
Rent	358,051			253,819
Depreciation and amortization	97,967			72,048
Marketing and promotional - related party	—			2,260,850
Professional fees	2,274,283			1,947,608
Other general and administrative	655,557			263,653
Total Operating Expenses	5,104,494			5,130,647
Operating Loss	(3,980,668)			(4,189,849)
Other Income (Expense)				
Interest and dividend income	22,432			11,209
Interest expense - related party	—			(587,294)
Change in unrealized gain (loss) on trading securitie	(1,181,085)			2,007,374
Gain (loss) on sale of marketable securities	(1,460,576)			5,989,218
Total Other Income (Expense)	(2,619,229)			7,420,507
Income (Loss) Before Income Taxes	(6,599,897)			3,230,658
Provision for income taxes	—			(1,040,000)
Income (Loss) from continuing operations	(6,599,897)			2,190,658
Discontinued Operations				
Loss from operations from discontinued operations	(1,205,988)			—
Loss on rescission of discontinued operations	(1,138,536)			—
Loss on discontinued operations	(2,344,524)			—
Net Income (Loss)	(8,944,421)			2,190,658
Per Share Amounts				
Income (Loss) from continuing operations				
Basic earnings per share	(0.04)			0.02
Diluted earnings per share	(0.04)			0.01
Loss on discontinuing operations				
Basic and Diluted earnings per share	(0.02)			—
Net Income (Loss)				
Basic earnings per share	(0.06)			0.02
Diluted earnings per share	(0.06)			0.01
Weighted Average Common Shares				
Basic	152,346,182			136,649,628
Diluted	152,346,182			164,052,726

When we look at the income statement, in 2014 it says there was a net income of $2.1 million. However, if we look closer at the income statement, SPYR had a $4.1 Million operating loss. It then had a gain in Sales of Marketable Securities of $6 million to offset this. We might be reassured, but the truth is that the $6 million should probably not be considered in your calculation of earnings. **If a company has an operating loss, then the company is not profitable.**

The following year in 2015, SPYR had a net loss of $8.9 Million. If data is in parenthesis then that means negative, meaning that SPYR's net loss is -8.9 (8.9). This is an example of management being able to make the 2014 earnings look better than they are by placing a 6 million dollar gain in "other income." You cannot always trust PE Ratios. As with SPYR, PE Ratios do not always show the real profits of a business. If the net income is positive but with an operating loss, this is a major red flag and needs to be investigated more.

Now looking at cash flows, we can see that SPYR had a net cash loss in operating activities of $2.8 million in 2014. This loss is not good, another major red flag. Below is the statement of **Cash Flows**:

Cash Flows

	2015		2014
Cash Flows From Operating Activities:			
Net income (loss) for the period	(8,944,421)		2,190,658
Adjustments to reconcile net income (loss) to net cash			
provided by (used in) operating activities:			
Loss on discontinued operations	2,344,524		—
Depreciation and amortization	97,967		72,048
Non-cash interest on notes payable, related parties	—		587,294
Common stock issued for employee compensation	796,168		987,500
Common stock issued for professional fees	1,265,133		—
Vesting of shares of common stock issued for services	61,250		—
Unrealized (gain) loss on trading securities	1,181,085		(2,007,374)
(Gain) loss on sale of trading securities	1,460,576		(5,989,218)
Deferred income tax expense	—		1,040,000
Increase in accounts receivables	(3,430)		—
Decrease in inventory	1,542		2,001
Decrease in prepaid expenses	5,286		(46,518)
Increase in capitalized licensing rights	(80,000)		—
Increase in other assets	(7,299)		—
Increase in accounts payable and accrued liabilities	32,321		33,172
Decrease in related party accounts payable	(262,494)		270,000
Net Cash Used for Operating Activities from Continuing Operations	(2,051,792)		(2,860,437)
Net Cash Used for Operating Activities from Discontinued Operations	(864,222)		—
Net Cash Used for Operating Activities	(2,916,014)		(2,860,437)
Cash Flows From Investing Activities:			
Purchases of trading securities	—		(1,402,035)
Purchases of available-for-sale securities	—		(590,000)
Prepayment on purchase of available-for-sale securities	—		43,750
Proceeds from sale of trading securities	3,060,675		8,579,373
Purchase of property and equipment	(214,752)		—
Purchase of intangible assets	(20,202)		(5,000)
Net Cash Provided by Investing Activities	2,825,721		6,626,088
Cash Flows From Financing Activities:			
Proceeds from sale of common stock	—		1,600,000
Net Cash Provided by Financing Activities	—		1,600,000
Net Cash Provided by Continuing and Discontinued Operations	(90,293)		5,365,651
Cash and cash equivalents at beginning of period	6,994,180		1,628,529
Cash and cash equivalents at end of period	6,903,887		6,994,180

Financial Statements from ("10-k," n.d.)

The lesson to be learned with SPYR is that even though the balance sheet looked conservative, it is still a horrible investment—especially with a book value of around $7.6 million and the entire company selling for $150 Million. If this company were selling for $3 million, it would still be a poor investment due to the fact that they do not make a profit. 5 years later SPYR is selling for $17 Million. You would have lost almost 90 percent of your investment, and it is easy to see why.

You might be wondering how a company like SPYR can sell for $150 million and then $17 million a few years later. Here is a quote from Benjamin Graham, Warren Buffett's mentor: "In the short run, the market is a voting machine, but in the long run, it is a weighing machine" (SeekingAlpha, 2019). This is a perfect explanation of the sometimes irrational behavior of the stock market.

To be fair to SPYR, if you had simply read a few pages in the annual report, they paint a clear picture of how bad it is. You need to read the annual reports of companies and be able to comprehend the business before investing in them. **Investing is more than financial statements, you must think about the business and its future.**

GME

I have never invested in GameStop, but as I was writing this book the drama with GameStop began. I figured I would add it to this section as an interesting example to show investors what not to do. A lot of the GME drama has nothing to do with investing, but I will quickly cover what happened with GameStop in January and early February of 2021.

Over the last 5 years, GameStop's revenue has been decreasing. From 2016 to 2020 revenue decreased almost 33 percent. At the business year's ending, 2/2/2019 and 2/1/2020, the company had an operating income of $-702 Million and $-400 Million respectively. Compared to the year ending 1/30/2016, GME had an operating income of $648 Million.

As a side note: each company has a different date they consider years. These are called **fiscal years**. So, GameStop's financial statement for year 2020 is really the business/fiscal year from 2/3/2019 to 2/1/2020. I am saying this to show that these results were not a product COVID-19. The last 3 quarters with COVID-19, the company had a $257 Million loss in operating income. The point is that GME's business has struggled for the last 5 years with or without COVID-19.

Looking below at the Balance Sheet of GameStop, it is not terrible; I would not say it is good, but it is not as bad as a lot of other stocks. Observe that at the end of fiscal year 2020 (2/1/2020) GameStop had a shareholders' equity or Book Value of $612 Million. However, if we take a deeper look at those assets, we see some doubts on the ability to get cash out of some of them. Remember what I said about a lot of assets being good until reached for? Some of these assets are probably exactly that. GameStop had $499 Million cash which is a good asset and we can probably count most of that. In the "current assets" line, they had $860 Million in total inventory, $142 Million in total receivables, $119 Million in prepaid expenses, and $25 million in other assets and discontinued operations; this amounts to a total of over $1.1 Billion in current assets. As an investor I would not count on getting all of that back. To be generous, let us say that GME gets half of that back, so subtract $550 Million from the Balance Sheet. There is no science to these calculations, I am just thinking/estimating. Looking at long term assets, GME has about $1.2 Billion in mostly property, plants, and equipment. Again, let us say they can get half of that back, so they lost another $600 Million.

Taking a look at the Balance sheet, at first it looks decent with $612 Million in Book Value, but when we look more closely at the assets and subtract the values we calculated above, $1.1 Billion, we find out GME's book value is probably more like $-500 Million in our opinion. Everyone will come up with different values for this. Maybe some people will think that all of those assets are good, I just like to lean on the conservative side. As the year went on, you can observe on the quarterly reports that the balance sheet gets worse and worse.

Since GameStop was struggling so badly, many people and especially quite a few hedge funds were shorting GameStop. **Shorting** means to bet that the price of a stock will go down. The farther it goes down the more money you make. Shorting is extremely risky, and I do not recommend trying it because you have a limited gain, and your losses are potentially unlimited. Plus, even if you are correct in your analysis that the company is overpriced, it could be years before it pays off and you will be losing more and more money.

Seeing such a high number of shorts, the people of Reddit decided they wanted to screw over the big hedge funds. (Reddit is a social media site that is more concentrated than twitter and people join different groups or subreddits, where they can chat about their opinions). Anyway, a group on Reddit called WallStreetBets decided that they wanted to stick it to these hedge funds by pushing the price up. The people on this page started buying the shares, in some cases Millions of dollars' worth. At the beginning of January 2021, GME stock was trading around $17. As people bought it, the stock more than doubled, and by mid-January it was over $40. By January 25th it was up over $70.

The problem with shorting is as the stock goes up you lose more and more money; the only way to stop the losses is to buy your shares back which causes the shares to go even higher. That is what happened—the hedge funds and shorters had to buy back shares to stop their losses, the people of Reddit and people watching the news all became stock experts overnight, so the buying continued. The next day, January 26th 2021, GME almost doubled to $146. The following day it more than doubled to $340, and at one point it was over $400 a share.

To show you how crazy this is, let us look at the market cap. The GameStop business that we were talking about earlier had $1.1 Billion in operating losses in the last 2 fiscal years, and a $257 Million operating loss the last 3 quarters. GME had a Book Value at the end of fiscal year 2020 of $650 Million, which we said was more like negative $500 Million. Looking at the last quarter's Book Value, it is at $332 Million and probably even lower than our $-500 Million real Book Value. So, if you were looking to buy this entire business how much would you pay for it?

Personally, I would not pay a dime for GameStop. I cannot imagine this business getting any better with competitors everywhere. Anyone can easily buy a game online from Amazon or Walmart and have it delivered the next day, or simply walk into Walmart and get the game cheaper than GameStop. For buying and downloading games online, GameStop has numerous competitors, such as Steam and GOG. Some people might be willing to pay $300 Million for the GameStop brand and its assets, hoping they can turn it around. However, that is not my game and I just do not know enough about GameStop to be able to picture the turnaround.

In July 2020, GME was selling for $4.00 a share which was about a $250 Million market cap. This had me a bit interested in it, but after looking at the company I came to the conclusion I presented above. I just could not dream up a turnaround for GameStop. Obviously, looking back now I wish I would have put in some money at $4.00 a share and multiplied my investment by 80 times; hindsight is 20/20. However, there is no way I could have predicted what happened. I believe my analysis on GME was correct so I can sleep easy. This was not a mistake like the other companies I bought. Also, it would have given me false confidence about my ability to gamble in the stock market.

Anyway, when GME was selling for $4.00 a share the company had a market cap of $250 Million. Maybe someone could invest in it. As it got up to $17 a share, the market cap jumped to over 1 Billion dollars. I do not think anyone could believe GameStop is worth that much. When it got up to over $300 a share the market cap was over $20 Billion dollars getting to a high of $24 Billion dollars! Obviously, GameStop is not worth this much money—a lot of traders thinking they are investors were going to get burned. As the stock keeps going up people think they are stock experts and buy. People see their friends making money and buy, and so on. Eventually, many people who have no idea what they are doing buying into GameStop at ridiculous prices are going to lose their hard-earned money. Which is already what happened when the stock dropped from a high of $400 to about $68 in a week. That is an 80% loss, mostly coming from people who truly thought they were investing and listening to all their friends telling them to buy. Here's Warren Buffett on bubbles, which is what GameStop and the companies like it are: "People start being interested in something because it's going up, not because they understand it or anything else. But the guy next door, who they know is dumber than they are, is getting rich and they aren't…And their spouse is saying can't you figure it out too? It is so contagious. So that's a permanent part of the system." (qtd. in Kim, 2018). Absolutely perfect explanation of a bubble.

The worst part of GameStop is people really thought they were investing. If your goal were to stick it to the hedge funds and gamble away your money, then sure go for it. I think it is still dumb but at least you know it is dumb and a gamble. The problem with the idea of sticking it to the hedge funds is sure you make the price of the stock go up and the hedge might lose a lot of money and might even go bankrupt, but at the end of the day the people in those funds are still going to be rich. The people you are really screwing over are all the average people you convinced to buy this stupid stock. When you sell a stock, someone must buy it. Even if you bought at $17 a share and sold at $400, great for you, but some average person just lost 80% of their life savings or more in less than a week. You did not "stick it to the hedge funds," you stuck it to the average Joe thinking they were investing.

If what I just wrote is a bit confusing, do not worry. The main takeaway is:
DO NOT BUY COMPANIES BECAUSE EVERYONE ELSE IS. DO NOT BUY A STOCK BECAUSE IT IS GOING UP.
Below are GameStop's Annual and Quarterly reports: (Values are in millions except for per share data)

GME Yearly Results
Income Statement

	2020	2019	2018	2017	2016
Total Revenue	6,466	8,285	8,547	7,965	9,364
Operating Expenses					
Cost of Revenue, Total	4,557	5,977	6,062	5,465	6,446
Selling/Gen/Admin Expense	1,861	1,886	1,914	1,857	2,077
Labor & Related Expense	--	--	--	--	30
Sell/Gen/Admin Expenses, Total	1,861	1,886	1,914	1,857	2,107
Depreciation/Amortization	--	106	122	137	157
Investment Income, Operating	1	3	2	5	2
Interest/Investment Income, Operating	1	3	2	5	2
Restructuring Charge	61	--	--	--	--
Impair-Assets Held for use	386	1,016	14	20	5
Other Unusual Expense (In)	--	--	-6	--	--
Unusual Expense (Income)	446	1,016	7	20	5
Total Operating Expense	6,866	8,987	8,108	7,483	8,716
Operating Income					
Total Operating Income	-400	-702	439	482	648
Non-Operating Income & Expenses					
Interest Expense, Net Non-Operating	-39	-57	-57	-54	-23
Interest Income, Non-Operating	11	6	2	1	0
Interest/Investment Income, Non-Operati	11	6	2	1	0
Income Before Tax	-427	-753	384	429	625
Income Taxes					
Provision for Income Taxes	38	64	154	124	222
Net Income After Taxes	-464	-818	230	305	403
Minority Interest & Equity in Affiliates					
Net Income Before Extra Items	-464	-818	230	305	403
Extraordinary Items					
Discontinued Operations	-9	122	-196	49	--
Extraordinary Item	0	23	--	--	--
Tax on Extraordinary Items	3	--	--	--	--
Total Extraordinary Items	-7	145	-196	49	--
Net Income					
Net Income	-471	-673	35	353	403
Adjustments to Net Income					
Income Available to Common Excl. Extra.	-464	-818	230	305	403
Income Available to Common Incl. Extra.	-471	-673	35	353	403
EPS Reconciliation					
Basic/Primary Weighted Average Shares	88	102	101	103	106
Basic/Primary EPS Excl. Extra. Items	-5.31	-8.01	2.27	2.94	3.8
Basic/Primary EPS Incl. Extra. Items	-5.38	-6.59	0.34	3.42	3.8
Dilution Adjustment	--	--	--	--	0
Diluted Weighted Average Shares	88	102	102	104	107
Diluted EPS Excl. Extra. Items	-5.31	-8.01	2.27	2.93	3.78
Diluted EPS Incl. Extra. Items	-5.38	-6.59	0.34	3.4	3.78
Common Stock Dividends					
DPS - Common Stock Primary Issue	0.38	1.52	1.52	1.48	1.44
Gross Dividend - Common Stock	39	156	156	155	154
Pro Forma Net Income					
Pro Forma Net Income	--	--	--	--	--
Supplemental Items					
Interest Expense, Supplemental	39	57	57	54	23
Depreciation, Supplemental	91	127	152	167	158
Normalized Income					
Total Special Items	455	1,016	7	20	5
Normalized Income Before Tax	29	263	391	448	630
Effect of Special Items on Income Taxes	159	356	3	6	2
Income Tax Exempt Impact of Special Item	197	420	156	130	224
Normalized Income After Tax	-168	-157	235	318	406
Normalized Income Avail to Common	-168	-157	235	318	406
Basic Normalized EPS	-1.92	-1.54	2.32	3.08	3.83
Diluted Normalized EPS	-1.92	-1.54	2.31	3.07	3.8

Balance Sheet

	2020	2019	2018	2017	2016
Assets					
Cash and Short Term Investments	499	1,624	854	669	450
Trade Accounts Receivable, Gross	35	45	49	40	--
Provision for Doubtful Accounts	-13	-4	-8	-6	--
Trade Accounts Receivable, Net	22	41	42	34	177
Other Receivables	120	94	97	187	--
Total Receivables, Net	142	134	139	221	177
Total Inventory	860	1,251	1,250	1,122	1,163
Prepaid Expenses	119	115	113	116	107
Restricted Cash - Current	0	3	0	--	--
Deferred Income Tax	--	--	--	--	0
Discontinued Operations - Current Assets	12	0	660	--	--
Other Current Assets	1	1	2	13	41
Other Current Assets, Total	14	4	663	13	41
Total Current Assets	1,634	3,128	3,018	2,141	1,938
Buildings	612	638	652	725	668
Land/Improvements	18	19	20	19	17
Other Property/Plant/Equipment	1,603	900	915	931	875
Property/Plant/Equipment - Gross	2,233	1,557	1,586	1,675	1,560
Accumulated Depreciation	-1,190	-1,236	-1,235	-1,204	-1,076
Property/Plant/Equipment - Net	1,043	321	351	471	485
Goodwill, Net	0	364	1,351	1,725	1,477
Intangibles, Gross	--	133	198	--	--
Accumulated Intangible Amortization	--	-100	-105	--	--
Intangibles, Net	--	34	93	507	330
Deferred Income Tax - Long Term Asset	83	147	158	59	39
Restricted Cash - Long Term	14	13	15	--	--
Other Long Term Assets	46	37	56	73	62
Total Assets	2,820	4,044	5,042	4,976	4,330
Liabilities					
Accounts Payable	381	1,052	892	617	632
Accrued Expenses	471	312	441	468	1,041
Notes Payable/Short Term Debt	0	0	0	0	0
Current Portion of Long-Term Debt/Capita	0	349	0	--	0
Customer Advances	117	124	132	132	--
Income Taxes Payable	35	73	101	203	121
Discontinued Operations	--	0	51	--	--
Other Current Liabilities	235	271	313	343	--
Other Current Liabilities, Total	386	468	598	677	121
Total Current Liabilities	1,238	2,181	1,931	1,762	1,794
Total Long Term Debt	420	472	818	815	345
Total Debt	420	821	818	815	346
Deferred Income Tax	--	0	5	23	30
Other Liabilities, Total	551	55	73	122	80
Total Liabilities	2,208	2,708	2,827	2,722	2,249
Shareholder Equity					
Common Stock	0	0	0	0	0
Additional Paid-In Capital	0	28	22	0	0
Retained Earnings (Accumulated Deficit)	690	1,363	2,180	2,301	2,170
Other Equity, Total	-79	-54	12	-47	-89
Total Equity	612	1,336	2,215	2,254	2,081
Total Liabilities & Shareholders' Equity	2,820	4,044	5,042	4,976	4,330
Total Common Shares Outstanding	64	102	101	101	103
Treasury Shares-Common Primary Issue	0	0	0	0	0

Cash Flows

	2020	2019	2018	2017	2016
Cash From Operating Activities					
Net Income	-471	-673	35	353	403
Depreciation/Depletion	96	127	152	167	158
Deferred Taxes	61	-4	-108	-37	-2
Unusual Items	397	917	397	44	8
Other Non-Cash Items	13	32	51	34	21
Non-Cash Items	410	949	448	78	29
Cash Taxes Paid, Supplemental	51	123	168	230	122
Cash Interest Paid, Supplemental	34	54	53	23	22
Accounts Receivable	-11	-34	36	-44	-58
Inventories	361	-45	-256	15	-49
Prepaid Expesnes	-72	-17	-26	-61	90
Payable/Accrued	-793	17	170	64	91
Changes in Working Capital	-511	-74	-92	-24	68
Total Cash from Operations	-415	325	435	537	657
Plus: Cash From Investing Activities					
Capital Expenditures	-79	-94	-113	-143	-173
Acquisition of Business	0	0	-9	-441	-268
Sale of Business	5	728	59	0	--
Other Investing Cash Flow	12	1	3	6	-4
Other Investment Cash Flow Items, Total	18	729	53	-435	-271
Total Cash from Investing	-61	636	-61	-578	-445
Cash From Financing Activities					
Financing Cash Flow Items	--	0	0	-9	4
Total Cash Dividends Paid	-41	-157	-155	-156	-154
Repurchase/Retirement Common	-199	0	-22	-63	-194
Common Stock, Net	-200	-5	-26	-63	-194
Options Exercised	--	--	--	-8	--
Issuance (Retirement) of Stock, Net	-200	-5	-26	-72	-194
Long Term Debt Issued	0	154	0	475	--
Long Term Debt Reduction	-405	-166	-395	-545	-465
Long Term Debt, Net	-405	-12	-395	-70	-465
Total Debt Issued	--	--	373	545	463
Issue (Retirement) of Debt, Net	-405	-12	-22	475	-2
Total Cash from Financing	-645	-175	-203	239	-346
Equals: Increase In Cash					
Foreign Exchange Effects	-7	-25	28	21	-26
Net Change in Cash	-1,127	761	200	219	-160
Net Cash - Begin Balance/Reserved for Fut	1,641	869	675	450	610
Net Cash - End Balance/Reserved for Futu	514	1,630	875	669	450
Depreciation, Supplemental	96	127	152	167	158
Cash Interest Paid, Supplemental	34	54	53	23	22
Cash Taxes Paid, Supplemental	51	123	168	230	122

Quarterly Results
Income Statement

	Q3 2021	Q2 2021	Q1 2021	Q4 2020	Q3 2020
Revenue & Gross Profit					
Total Revenue	1,005	942	1,021	2,194	1,439
Operating Expenses					
Cost of Revenue, Total	728	690	739	1,597	997
Sell/Gen/Admin Expenses, Total	360	348	386	555	438
Depreciation/Amortization	--	--	--	--	24
Investment Income, Operating	0	0	0	2	-1
Interest/Investment Income, Operating	0	0	0	2	-1
Restructuring Charge	--	--	--	24	14
Impair-Assets Held for use	0	1	4	10	11
Unusual Expense (Income)	-21	-10	4	35	26
Loss (Gain)/Sale Assets (Operations)	-21	-11	--	--	--
Other Operating Expense, Total	--	--	--	-69	--
Other, Net	--	--	--	-69	--
Total Operating Expense	1,068	1,028	1,129	2,119	1,484
Operating Income					
Total Operating Income	-63	-86	-108	75	-46
Non-Operating Income & Expenses					
Interest Expense, Net Non-Operating	-10	-8	-8	-8	-8
Interest Income, Non-Operating	0	0	1	1	2
Interest/Investment Income, Non-Operati	0	0	1	1	2
Income Before Tax	-73	-93	-115	69	-52
Income Taxes					
Provision for Income Taxes	-54	18	50	44	32
Net Income After Taxes	-19	-111	-165	25	-83
Minority Interest & Equity in Affiliates					
Net Income Before Extra Items	-19	-111	-165	25	-83
Extraordinary Items					
Discontinued Operations	0	0	-1	-6	0
Extraordinary Item	--	--	--	0	--
Tax on Extraordinary Items	--	0	0	2	0
Total Extraordinary Items	0	0	-1	-4	0
Net Income					
Net Income	-19	-111	-166	21	-83
Adjustments to Net Income					
Income Available to Common Excl. Extra.	-19	-111	-165	25	-83
Income Available to Common Incl. Extra. I	-19	-111	-166	21	-83
EPS Reconciliation					
Basic/Primary Weighted Average Shares	65	65	65	66	82
Basic/Primary EPS Excl. Extra. Items	-0.29	-1.71	-2.56	0.38	-1.01
Basic/Primary EPS Incl. Extra. Items	-0.29	-1.71	-2.57	0.32	-1.02
Diluted Weighted Average Shares	65	65	65	66	82
Diluted EPS Excl. Extra. Items	-0.29	-1.71	-2.56	0.38	-1.01
Diluted EPS Incl. Extra. Items	-0.29	-1.71	-2.57	0.32	-1.02
Common Stock Dividends					
DPS - Common Stock Primary Issue	0	0	0	0	0
Gross Dividend - Common Stock	--	--	--	--	0
Pro Forma Net Income					
Pro Forma Net Income	--	--	--	--	--
Supplemental Items					
Interest Expense, Supplemental	10	8	8	8	8
Depreciation, Supplemental	19	20	22	26	24
Normalized Income					
Total Special Items	-21	-10	4	43	27
Normalized Income Before Tax	-94	-104	-111	111	-25
Effect of Special Items on Income Taxes	-7	-4	1	15	9
Income Tax Exempt Impact of Special Item	-61	14	52	59	41
Normalized Income After Tax	-33	-118	-163	53	-66
Normalized Income Avail to Common	-33	-118	-163	53	-66
Basic Normalized EPS	-0.5	-1.81	-2.52	0.8	-0.8
Diluted Normalized EPS	-0.5	-1.81	-2.52	0.8	-0.8

Balance Sheet

	Q3 2021	Q2 2021	Q1 2021	Q4 2020	Q3 2020
Assets					
Cash and Short Term Investments	446	735	570	499	290
Trade Accounts Receivable, Net	78	83	87	142	146
Total Receivables, Net	78	83	87	142	146
Total Inventory	861	475	655	860	1,287
Prepaid Expenses	127	76	97	119	126
Restricted Cash - Current	141	11	0	0	0
Discontinued Operations - Current Assets	0	0	9	12	13
Other Current Assets	--	--	2	1	1
Other Current Assets, Total	141	11	12	14	14
Total Current Assets	1,652	1,380	1,420	1,634	1,863
Other Property/Plant/Equipment	1,368	1,396	1,429	1,466	1,518
Property/Plant/Equipment - Gross	1,368	1,396	1,429	1,466	1,518
Accumulated Depreciation	-1,175	-1,177	-1,172	-1,190	-1,230
Property/Plant/Equipment - Net	860	909	963	1,043	1,045
Goodwill, Net	--	--	0	0	0
Deferred Income Tax - Long Term Asset	29	29	29	83	158
Restricted Cash - Long Term	16	13	14	14	14
Other Long Term Assets	45	45	44	46	66
Total Assets	2,601	2,375	2,469	2,820	3,146
Liabilities					
Accounts Payable	440	256	212	381	710
Accrued Expenses	867	790	753	856	862
Notes Payable/Short Term Debt	25	35	135	0	0
Current Portion of Long-Term Debt/Capita	245	221	417	0	0
Discontinued Operations	--	0	--	--	0
Other Current Liabilities	--	9	2	1	1
Other Current Liabilities, Total	--	9	2	1	1
Total Current Liabilities	1,577	1,312	1,520	1,238	1,574
Total Long Term Debt	216	216	0	420	419
Total Debt	486	472	552	420	419
Other Liabilities, Total	477	495	514	551	536
Total Liabilities	2,269	2,023	2,034	2,208	2,529
Shareholder Equity					
Common Stock	0	0	0	0	0
Additional Paid-In Capital	5	3	1	0	0
Retained Earnings (Accumulated Deficit)	394	413	525	690	689
Other Equity, Total	-67	-64	-91	-79	-72
Total Equity	332	352	435	612	617
Total Liabilities & Shareholders' Equity	2,601	2,375	2,469	2,820	3,146
Total Common Shares Outstanding	65	65	65	64	68
Treasury Shares-Common Primary Issue	0	0	0	0	0

Cash Flows

	Q3 2021	Q2 2021	Q1 2021	Q4 2020	Q3 2020
Cash From Operating Activities					
Net Income	-296	-277	-166	-471	-492
Depreciation/Depletion	61	42	22	96	70
Deferred Taxes	45	45	45	61	-12
Unusual Items	-26	-5	4	397	378
Other Non-Cash Items	9	4	2	13	-5
Non-Cash Items	-17	-1	7	410	373
Accounts Receivable	66	61	54	-11	-7
Inventories	12	394	196	361	-62
Prepaid Expesnes	9	72	28	-72	-55
Payable/Accrued	79	-194	-274	-793	-472
Changes in Working Capital	165	335	43	-511	-595
Total Cash from Operations	-41	144	-49	-415	-655
Cash From Investing Activities					
Capital Expenditures	-33	-18	-7	-79	-61
Acquisition of Business	--	--	--	0	--
Sale of Business	--	--	--	5	5
Sale of Fixed Assets	96	52	--	--	--
Other Investing Cash Flow	0	2	1	12	-1
Other Investment Cash Flow Items, Total	96	54	1	18	5
Total Cash from Investing	63	36	-6	-61	-57
Cash From Financing Activities					
Financing Cash Flow Items	-1	-1	-1	--	--
Total Cash Dividends Paid	0	0	0	-41	-41
Repurchase/Retirement Common	0	0	--	-199	-177
Common Stock, Net	0	0	--	-200	-178
Issuance (Retirement) of Stock, Net	0	0	--	-200	-178
Long Term Debt Issued	197	174	150	0	0
Long Term Debt Reduction	-130	-120	-17	-405	-405
Long Term Debt, Net	67	53	133	-405	-405
Issue (Retirement) of Debt, Net	67	53	133	-405	-405
Total Cash from Financing	66	52	132	-645	-623
Equals: Increase In Cash					
Foreign Exchange Effects	1	14	-6	-7	-2
Net Change in Cash	89	245	70	-1,127	-1,336
Net Cash - Begin Balance/Reserved for Fut	514	514	514	1,641	1,641
Net Cash - End Balance/Reserved for Futu	603	759	584	514	304
Depreciation, Supplemental	61	42	22	96	70

GameStops financial reports taken from Charles Schwabs Website. (Charles Schwab | A modern approach to investing & retirement, n.d.)

Pre-Intelligent Investor Overview

There is a stat online that says 90% of investors lose money. I do not think this is true, but I would certainly believe that 90% or more of day traders lose money. Day traders are constantly buying companies that are losing billions of dollars a year, plus the cost of buying and selling stocks. Most people just want to get rich quick so they invest their money in risky companies that they heard might double in a month. Jeff Bezos asked Warren Buffett why everyone does not copy his investing strategy, Buffett's reply was "Because nobody wants to get rich slow" (qtd. in Mohamed, 2020). That is why most people lose money in the stock market. I was certainly on my way to becoming one of these 90%. Before reading *The Intelligent Investor*, I bought 8 companies like those first three I showed you—LNCO, PPCB, and SPYR—all resulting in huge percentage losses. All of them looked just like those three, only with a different company name and business. **DO NOT INVEST IN COMPANIES LIKE THOSE. DO NOT BUY COMPANIES THAT LOSE MILLIONS/BILLIONS OF DOLLARS A YEAR.** If you are going to invest money into a company, you need to understand the business and be able to imagine the company's future 5, 10, 25 years down the road.

Section 4: Post-Intelligent Investor

After reading *The Intelligent Investor*, you will learn the most basic and most important ideas about investing in the stock market. The most basic idea is "A stock is not just a ticker symbol or an electronic blip; it is an ownership interest in an actual business, with an underlying value that does not depend on its share price." – Benjamin Graham, *The Intelligent Investor* (1985, p. xx). You must be aware that you are buying a business when you buy a stock. You need to understand and value that business before buying the stock.

Another main idea from *The Intelligent Investor* is that the stock market is there to serve you, not instruct you. Graham used an imaginary guy named Mr. Market to describe the stock market. Mr. Market comes to you every Monday-Friday and for 6 and a half hours he is constantly giving you prices of all the companies and he does not mind if you say no to everyone. However, Mr. Market is very emotional some days and sometimes years. Mr. Market can be very happy and does not see how anything can go wrong and his prices just keep going up and up. Other times Mr. Market is very depressed and sees the world falling apart and will continue to offer lower and lower prices for his companies. The more depressed Mr. Market is, the lower the prices and the better it is for the investor. Moral of the story is stocks become less risky when the prices go down and more risky when the prices go up. Take advantage of the overly emotional Mr. Market.

In *Old Charlie's Almanack*, Charlie discusses herd behavior. Herd behavior is why markets go up and down so drastically. Most people feel more comfortable going with the crowd, whatever the new style, fad, or the new "hot" stock. So, when people start to panic, everyone starts to panic. If you cannot control your emotions and go against the crowd, you should not be buying your own stocks. You must think for yourself to be an investor.

After reading *The Intelligent Investor* you will be looking for cheap companies with low book values and low price-to-earnings ratios. What Warren Buffett learned throughout the years is that it is better to buy a great company at a decent price than a bad or mediocre company at a great price. Charlie Munger helped Warren with this concept. Below I will show some examples of great companies and also some cigar butts.

AAPL

I talked earlier about Apple, but I will quickly explain more thoughts on why Apple was such a great investment in 2015. In 2015/2016, Apple was selling in the range of 10-14 Times earnings. Meaning as an investor you are buying a company with earnings yield of around 7-10%. In 2015 Apple had net income of 54 Billion dollars, with a PE of 10-14; it was selling between $540-700 Billion. Apple's Balance sheet was rock solid with about $110 Billion of Net tangible assets. That is a very good amount of tangible assets for a tech company. On top of this, Apple was paying over $11 Billion in dividends, or about 2% of its market cap, and bought back $35 Billion in stock. With the buyback, that means you now own about 6% more of the company than you did the previous year. If Apple continued to pay dividends and buyback shares at this rate, you could expect about an 8% return. That return would accrue even if Apple never grew earnings, which I would say is very doubtful over a long period of time. Consider Apple's 8% return compared to the treasury rate, which was about 2.3% in 2015, and the S&P, which was a little over 20 PE or a little less than a 5% earnings yield.

Now you should start thinking about the company. Apple has great products; the iPhone might be the greatest product ever made. Adults, kids, teenagers are hooked on their phones. It has made the world we live in much easier in many ways—our phones have a quality camera, speaker, GPS system, a high-powered search engine, e-mail, calculator, timer, games, millions of different apps, and a host of other great features. On top of this, people love their iPhones, as they continue to be highly-rated by consumers. Many people, given the option of a $1,000 dollar iPhone or a free any other phone, will pay for the iPhone. In 2015, Apple sold 231 Million iPhones. When I think about the whole world, there's 7 Billion+ humans; if Apple could just sell an iPhone to $1/7^{th}$ of the population that could be 1 Billion phones in a year. With the population growing every year I do not think 1 Billion iPhones is impossible. However, I know this is many years away and certainly a high estimate. The key point is that Apple can continue to sell many more phones.

Apple has numerous other great products, the iPhone just being the biggest. Another major growth segment for Apple is their services; revenue is increasing at a high rate with excellent profit margins. So, you go down the line and you try to paint a picture of the future. It was easy to see the future was bright with Apple. I bought my shares of Apple before Buffett, which made me feel smart... However, he got a better price. I had just started learning about Warren Buffett at this time and was not able to figure out how good this investment opportunity was. As I stated earlier, I kept buying and selling Apple and was able to get a solid return, but I could have made a lot more money if I had simply put all my money into Apple and held it forever. The moral of this story is when you get a big fat pitch to hit, do not put a little bit of your money in and play with it. Unload the bank account, hit the pitch hard, and just watch your money grow.

After I had read *The Intelligent Investor*, Apple's stock price had gone up and was now selling for 15- or 16-times earnings while also trading at around 6-times book value. At this point I thought that Apple was overpriced. *The Intelligent Investor* teaches you to buy companies with a Price to earnings (PE) lower than 10 and a Price to book (PB) of less than 1. In the 1900s there were plenty of companies like this and you could get a collection of a dozen companies and almost guarantee a decent return. However, those days are gone, and you need to be able to expand your investing horizon. What is more important than book value is how much cash the company is going to return to you in terms of dividends, buying back shares, and retaining earnings from today to judgment day. Apple has done a tremendous job in those categories. In 2017, Apple returned $12.7 Billion in dividends, and $33 Billion in share buy backs. Selling for around $750 Billion, that was about a 6% cash return for investors. Apple was not selling cheap, but you could buy an excellent company for a fair price. Apple has a very stable base of customers; they have continuously been able to bring in more users and keep users, and their customer satisfaction numbers are very good. For example, Apple's personal computers lead the U.S in costumer satisfaction in 2018 and 2019 (Owen, 2019). Also, Apple lead customer satisfaction in cellular devices in 2020 (Clover, 2020).

Today Apple is selling for 2.3 Trillion dollars and in 2020 they earned 57 Billion dollars. That is an earnings yield of only 2.5%. It is still a great company, everything I said above still applies, and I think their position has only gotten better these last few years. However, I can now find better opportunities than Apple at 2.5%. My gf still has shares of Apple because we are going to hold them forever, but I am not buying Apple at these levels. Nonetheless, with the 10-yr treasury at only 1%, I do not think buying Apple is a bad investment. 2.5% is much better than 1% and Apple is going to return a little more than 2.5% percent over the next 10 years by increasing earnings and buying back shares. Still, Apple is probably not going to yield too much higher than that 2.5%. I would be happy if Apple returned 5% over the next 5 years from its current levels.

The S&P 500 is selling for 38 PE; this is an earnings yield of 2.63%. Currently the S&P 500 has a higher earnings yield than Apple, but I think Apple will outperform the S&P 500 at these levels due to being a superior company compared to the average company. Also, Apple is increasing their earnings per share for shareholders at a higher rate than the average U.S company. But it is certainly close. This is a very small margin of safety to beat the S&P at current levels.

However, if Apple dropped 90% tomorrow, I would sell all my stocks and put it all in Apple. Apple would have an excellent return on investment from those levels. **Remember, when buying stock you want the stock market to go down not up**. This is a very hard concept for humans to understand.

Below are Apple's last 5 years financial statements:

(Values are in millions except for per share data)

Income Statement

	2020	2019	2018	2017	2016
Revenue & Gross Profit					
Total Revenue	274,515	260,174	265,595	229,234	215,639
Operating Expenses					
Cost of Revenue, Total	169,559	161,782	163,756	141,048	131,376
Selling/Gen/Admin Expense	19,916	18,245	15,043	13,597	12,642
Labor & Related Expense	--	--	1,662	1,664	1,552
Sell/Gen/Admin Expenses, Total	19,916	18,245	16,705	15,261	14,194
Research & Development	18,752	16,217	14,236	11,581	10,045
Total Operating Expense	208,227	196,244	194,697	167,890	155,615
Operating Income					
Total Operating Income	66,288	63,930	70,898	61,344	60,024
Non-Operating Income & Expenses					
Interest Expense, Net Non-Operating	-2,873	-3,576	-3,240	-2,323	-1,456
Interest Income, Non-Operating	3,763	4,961	5,686	5,201	3,999
Interest/Investment Income, Non-Operating	3,763	4,961	5,686	5,201	3,999
Other Non-Operation Income (Expense)	-87	422	-441	-133	-1,195
Other, Net	-87	422	-441	-133	-1,195
Income Before Tax	67,091	65,737	72,903	64,089	61,372
Income Taxes					
Provision for Income Taxes	9,680	10,481	11,872	15,738	15,685
Net Income After Taxes	57,411	55,256	61,031	48,351	45,687
Minority Interest & Equity in Affiliates					
Net Income Before Extra Items	57,411	55,256	61,031	48,351	45,687
Extraordinary Items					
Extraordinary Item	--	--	-1,500	--	--
Total Extraordinary Items	--	--	-1,500	--	--
Net Income					
Net Income	57,411	55,256	59,531	48,351	45,687
Adjustments to Net Income					
Income Available to Common Excl. Extra. Items	57,411	55,256	61,031	48,351	45,687
Income Available to Common Incl. Extra. Items	57,411	55,256	59,531	48,351	45,687
EPS Reconciliation					
Basic/Primary Weighted Average Shares	17,352	18,471	19,822	20,869	21,883
Basic/Primary EPS Excl. Extra. Items	3.31	2.99	3.08	2.32	2.09
Basic/Primary EPS Incl. Extra. Items	3.31	2.99	3	2.32	2.09
Diluted Weighted Average Shares	17,528	18,596	20,000	21,007	22,001
Diluted EPS Excl. Extra. Items	3.28	2.97	3.05	2.3	2.08
Diluted EPS Incl. Extra. Items	3.28	2.97	2.98	2.3	2.08
Common Stock Dividends					
DPS - Common Stock Primary Issue	0.8	0.75	0.68	0.6	0.55
Gross Dividend - Common Stock	14,087	14,129	13,735	12,563	11,965
Pro Forma Net Income					
Pro Forma Net Income	--	--	--	--	--
Supplemental Items					
Interest Expense, Supplemental	2,873	3,576	3,240	2,323	1,456
Depreciation, Supplemental	11,056	12,547	10,903	8,200	8,300
Normalized Income					
Normalized Income Before Tax	67,091	65,737	72,903	64,089	61,372
Income Tax Exempt Impact of Special Items	9,680	10,481	11,872	15,738	15,685
Normalized Income After Tax	57,411	55,256	61,031	48,351	45,687
Normalized Income Avail to Common	57,411	55,256	61,031	48,351	45,687
Basic Normalized EPS	3.31	2.99	3.08	2.32	2.09
Diluted Normalized EPS	3.28	2.97	3.05	2.3	2.08

Balance Sheet

	2020	2019	2018	2017	2016
Assets					
Cash	17,773	12,204	11,575	7,982	8,601
Cash & Equivalents	20,243	36,640	14,338	12,307	11,883
Short Term Investments	52,927	51,713	40,388	53,892	46,671
Cash and Short Term Investments	90,943	100,557	66,301	74,181	67,155
Trade Accounts Receivable, Gross	--	--	--	--	15,807
Provision for Doubtful Accounts	--	--	--	--	-53
Trade Accounts Receivable, Net	16,120	22,926	23,186	17,874	15,754
Other Receivables	21,325	22,878	25,809	17,799	13,545
Total Receivables, Net	37,445	45,804	48,995	35,673	29,299
Total Inventory	4,061	4,106	3,956	4,855	2,132
Restricted Cash - Current	36	23	--	--	--
Other Current Assets	11,228	12,329	12,087	13,936	8,283
Other Current Assets, Total	11,264	12,352	12,087	13,936	8,283
Total Current Assets	143,713	162,819	131,339	128,645	106,869
Buildings	10,283	9,075	8,205	7,279	6,517
Land/Improvements	17,952	17,085	16,216	13,587	10,185
Machinery/Equipment	75,291	69,797	65,982	54,210	44,543
Other Property/Plant/Equipment	8,570	--	--	--	--
Property/Plant/Equipment - Gross	112,096	95,957	90,403	75,076	61,245
Accumulated Depreciation	-66,760	-58,579	-49,099	-41,293	-34,235
Property/Plant/Equipment - Net	45,336	37,378	41,304	33,783	27,010
Goodwill, Net	--	--	--	--	5,414
Intangibles, Gross	--	--	--	--	9,012
Accumulated Intangible Amortization	--	--	--	--	-5,806
Intangibles, Net	--	--	--	--	3,206
Long Term Investments - Other	100,887	105,341	170,799	194,714	170,430
Long Term Investments	100,887	105,341	170,799	194,714	170,430
Restricted Cash - Long Term	1,737	1,357	--	--	--
Other Long Term Assets	32,215	31,621	22,283	18,177	8,757
Total Assets	323,888	338,516	365,725	375,319	321,686
Liabilities					
Accounts Payable	42,296	46,236	55,888	44,242	37,294
Accrued Expenses	1,436	--	--	--	20,951
Notes Payable/Short Term Debt	4,996	5,980	11,964	11,977	8,105
Current Portion of Long-Term Debt/Capital Liab	8,797	10,260	8,784	6,496	3,500
Customer Advances	6,643	5,522	5,966	7,548	8,080
Other Current Liabilities	41,224	37,720	33,327	30,551	1,076
Other Current Liabilities, Total	47,867	43,242	39,293	38,099	9,156
Total Current Liabilities	105,392	105,718	115,929	100,814	79,006
Capital Lease Obligations	637	--	--	--	--
Total Long Term Debt	99,304	91,807	93,735	97,207	75,427
Total Debt	113,097	108,047	114,483	115,680	87,032
Deferred Income Tax	--	--	--	31,504	26,019
Other Liabilities, Total	53,853	50,503	48,914	11,747	12,985
Total Liabilities	258,549	248,028	258,578	241,272	193,437
Shareholder Equity					
Common Stock	50,779	45,174	40,201	35,867	31,251
Retained Earnings (Accumulated Deficit)	14,966	45,898	70,400	98,330	96,364
Unrealized Gain (Loss)	1,846	707	-3,209	328	1,174
Cumulative Translation Adjustment	-1,375	-1,463	-1,055	-354	-578
Other Comprehensive Income	-877	172	810	-124	38
Other Equity, Total	-2,252	-1,291	-245	-478	-540
Total Equity	65,339	90,488	107,147	134,047	128,249
Total Liabilities & Shareholders' Equity	323,888	338,516	365,725	375,319	321,686
otal Common Shares Outstanding	16,977	17,773	19,020	20,505	21,345
Treasury Shares-Common Primary Issue	0	0	0	0	0

Cash Flows

	2020	2019	2018	2017	2016
Cash From Operating Activities					
Net Income	57,411	55,256	59,531	48,351	45,687
Depreciation/Depletion	11,056	12,547	10,903	10,157	10,505
Deferred Taxes	-215	-340	-32,590	5,966	4,938
Other Non-Cash Items	6,732	5,416	4,896	4,674	4,696
Non-Cash Items	6,732	5,416	4,896	4,674	4,696
Cash Taxes Paid, Supplemental	9,501	15,263	10,417	11,591	10,444
Cash Interest Paid, Supplemental	3,002	3,423	3,022	2,092	1,316
Accounts Receivable	8,470	3,176	-13,332	-6,347	476
Inventories	-127	-289	828	-2,723	217
Other Assets	-9,588	873	-423	-5,318	1,055
Accounts Payable	-4,062	-1,923	9,175	8,966	2,117
Changes in Working Capital	5,690	-3,488	34,694	-4,923	405
Total Cash from Operations	80,674	69,391	77,434	64,225	66,231
Cash From Investing Activities					
Capital Expenditures	-7,309	-10,495	-13,313	-12,451	-12,734
Acquisition of Business	-1,524	-624	-721	-329	-297
Sale/Maturity of Investment	120,483	98,724	104,072	126,465	111,794
Purchase of Investments	-115,148	-40,631	-73,227	-160,007	-143,816
Other Investing Cash Flow	-791	-1,078	-745	-124	-924
Other Investment Cash Flow Items, Total	3,020	56,391	29,379	-33,995	-33,243
Total Cash from Investing	-4,289	45,896	16,066	-46,446	-45,977
Cash From Financing Activities					
Financing Cash Flow Items	-3,760	-2,922	-2,527	-1,874	-1,570
Total Cash Dividends Paid	-14,081	-14,119	-13,712	-12,769	-12,150
Sale/Issuance of Common	880	781	669	555	495
Repurchase/Retirement Common	-72,358	-66,897	-72,738	-32,900	-29,722
Common Stock, Net	-71,478	-66,116	-72,069	-32,345	-29,227
Issuance (Retirement) of Stock, Net	-71,478	-66,116	-72,069	-32,345	-29,227
Short Term Debt, Net	-963	-5,977	-37	3,852	-397
Long Term Debt, Net	16,091	6,963	6,969	28,662	24,954
Total Debt Reduction	-12,629	-8,805	-6,500	-3,500	-2,500
Issue (Retirement) of Debt, Net	2,499	-7,819	432	29,014	22,057
Total Cash from Financing	-86,820	-90,976	-87,876	-17,974	-20,890
Equals: Increase In Cash					
Net Change in Cash	-10,435	24,311	5,624	-195	-636
Net Cash - Begin Balance/Reserved for Future U	50,224	25,913	20,289	20,484	21,120
Net Cash - End Balance/Reserved for Future Us	39,789	50,224	25,913	20,289	20,484
Depreciation, Supplemental	11,056	12,547	10,903	10,157	10,505
Cash Interest Paid, Supplemental	3,002	3,423	3,022	2,092	1,316
Cash Taxes Paid, Supplemental	9,501	15,263	10,417	11,591	10,444

Apple's financial reports taken from Charles Schwab's Website. (Charles
Schwab | A modern approach to investing & retirement, n.d.)

FSLR

This was the first company I bought after reading *The Intelligent Investor* and it was purely a "value" stock. FSLR is the company First Solar and they are a manufacturer of solar panels. I thought and still do think that solar energy is the energy of the future. So, I searched for a cheap solar company and found First Solar. In 2017 First Solar was selling for around $3 Billion, which means the market cap was around $3 Billion. The stock was selling for less than $30 a share. Looking at the Balance sheet from 2016 the company had $6.8 Billion in Assets and only $1.6 Billion in Liabilities, for a Book Value of $5.2 Billion. On top of that, the company had $1.3 Billion cash and $1.9 Billion in cash and short-term investments. With only $160 Million in goodwill and intangibles, First Solar's Net Tangible Book Value was still over $5 Billion. Therefore, by buying shares you are buying a company that has assets worth $5 Billion. Considering it is selling at only $3 Billion, this is a good start. Again, some of the assets are probably good until reached for, so we need to take a deeper look at the company.

However, evaluating companies is more than just looking at their Balance sheets. I knew that back then but not to the same degree I know now. So, I checked out FSLR and it seemed like they had good products and were about to come out with an even better product—the Series 6 Panel. The company's management were optimistic about the future. I thought FSLR could earn somewhere around 500 Million dollars a year soon. My predictions were way off. For the years 2016, 2017, 2018, 2019, FSLR's operating income was hit or miss. Indeed, the income was -568 M, 178 M, 40M, -162M, respectively. For those same years, the net income was -416M, -166M, 144M, -111M. You might be thinking *dang another bad investment*. My thought process was not nearly correct in terms of income, but since I bought at such a good price it was my first great investment gain. I bought my FSLR shares for around $29 a share and sold them for over $70 a share—a return of around 175% in just a little over a year. The stock since then has gone up and down, back all the way to the mid-30s to now back in the 100s.

Today I currently think First Solar is overvalued. The company is selling for $10 Billion dollars ($10 Billion market Cap). The company's most recent Book value in Q3 2020 was about $5.4 Billion: $7 Billion in Assets minus $1.6 Billion in Liabilities. For Tangible Assets, subtract the $72 Million from intangibles and goodwill, so call it $5.3 Billion. Next, looking through the Balance Sheet, subtract anything you are not comfortable with to give you a more conservative estimated book value. In current assets for Q3 2020, First Solar has $1.6 Billion in cash and short-term investments. I would say that is a pretty good asset. Then, First Solar has about 900 Million dollars in total inventory, prepaid expenses, restricted cash-current, discontinued operations-current, other assets. For those assets, I would subtract half, so $450 Million. Again, there is no exact reasoning behind this other than I think some of these assets are good until reached for. Once reached for, they may not be so good.

In long-term assets, FSLR has $2.9 Billion in property, plants, and equipment. I doubt we could sell all these assets for that price, but I do think the plants they have are making great Series 6 panels, so I will give it to them. Additional long-term assets include around $1.2 Billion in deferred income tax, restricted cash, and other long-term assets. I will say maybe we could get half of these if asked for. So, my more conservative estimate for FSLR's book value would be around $4.2 Billion: Take $5.4 Billion and subtract $75 Million in intangibles, $450 Million current assets, and $600 Million in long term assets.

I still like FSLR's Series 6 solar panels, but I just cannot be certain that the company can consistently make a profit. The last 4 years combined, they have had an operating loss of $512 Million. However, the last three quarters they have had a positive operating income, for a total of $260 Million. I do not know what First Solar's earnings or revenue will look like over the next year let alone the next 5 to 10 years, which makes it very hard to invest in. On top of this uncertainty, the company has issued about 4 Million shares over the last 5 years. With about 100 million shares, that means they gave away 4% of the company, which I hate. If I were to invest in FSLR again, it would be a "value" play because I cannot paint a picture of the company's future earnings, even though I like the products and love the industry. I think the Book Value is $4 Billion-ish. So, if the market cap was less than $3 Billion, I would maybe be tempted to put in about 10% of my capital, because I believe solar energy is the future and they have a great product. I would hope they could profit $300 Million a year soon. This of course is if I could not find anything better. I would never put a big chunk of my capital into any company if I were not confident in the company's earnings over a 5–10-year basis. I still believe solar energy has a bright future and FSLR makes good panels, but they just cannot seem to make a consistent profit. To buy a company like this, it would need to be at a steep discount to book value.

In FSLR I made a mistake in my judgment, but since I bought the company at a good price, I did not lose money. Rather I made a decent amount of money. This is what we call the margin of safety. Do not invest in a company that you need a calculator to tell you if you will make a profit or not. Below are FSLR's yearly and quarterly financial statements:

(Values are in millions except for per share data)

Yearly Statements
Income Statement

	2019	2018	2017	2016	2015
Revenue & Gross Profit					
Total Revenue	3,063	2,244	2,941	2,905	4,113
Operating Expenses					
Cost of Revenue, Total	2,514	1,852	2,392	2,266	2,980
Selling/Gen/Admin Expense	227	246	223	245	242
Labor & Related Expense	24	22	23	18	30
Sell/Gen/Admin Expenses, Total	251	268	245	263	272
Research & Development	97	84	89	125	131
Restructuring Charge	0	0	37	744	0
Litigation	363	--	--	--	--
Impair-Assets Held for use	--	0	0	75	0
Unusual Expense (Income)	363	0	37	819	0
Total Operating Expense	3,225	2,204	2,763	3,473	3,382
Operating Income					
Total Operating Income	-162	40	178	-568	730
Non-Operating Income & Expenses					
Interest Expense, Non-Operating	-21	-23	-27	-26	-19
Interest Capital, Non-Operating	3	6	2	6	12
Interest Expense, Net Non-Operating	-19	-17	-26	-21	-7
Interest Income, Non-Operating	49	60	36	25	23
Investment Income, Non-Operating	-6	-9	-9	-14	-7
Interest/Investment Income, Non-Operating	43	51	27	11	16
Other Non-Operation Income (Expense)	18	39	23	40	-6
Other, Net	18	39	23	40	-6
Income Before Tax	-120	113	202	-537	733
Income Taxes					
Provision for Income Taxes	-5	14	-36	23	32
Net Income After Taxes	-115	99	238	-560	701
Minority Interest & Equity in Affiliates					
Equity in Affiliates	0	35	4	144	-108
Net Income Before Extra Items	-115	134	242	-416	593
Extraordinary Items					
Extraordinary Item	--	10	-408	--	--
Net Income					
Net Income	-115	144	-166	-416	593
Adjustments to Net Income					
Income Available to Common Excl. Extra. Items	-115	134	242	-416	593
Income Available to Common Incl. Extra. Items	-115	144	-166	-416	593
EPS Reconciliation					
Basic/Primary Weighted Average Shares	105	105	104	103	101
Basic/Primary EPS Excl. Extra. Items	-1.09	1.28	2.32	-4.05	5.88
Basic/Primary EPS Incl. Extra. Items	-1.09	1.38	-1.59	-4.05	5.88
Diluted Weighted Average Shares	105	106	104	103	102
Diluted EPS Excl. Extra. Items	-1.09	1.26	2.32	-4.05	5.83
Diluted EPS Incl. Extra. Items	-1.09	1.36	-1.59	-4.05	5.83
Common Stock Dividends					
DPS - Common Stock Primary Issue	--	--	--	--	0
Gross Dividend - Common Stock	0	0	0	0	0
Pro Forma Net Income					
Pro Forma Net Income	--	--	--	--	--
Supplemental Items					
Interest Expense, Supplemental	48	49	26	21	7
Interest Capitalized, Supplemental	-3	-6	-2	-6	-12
Depreciation, Supplemental	195	121	107	221	249
Normalized Income					
Total Special Items	363	0	37	819	0
Normalized Income Before Tax	243	113	239	282	733
Effect of Special Items on Income Taxes	127	0	13	287	0
Income Tax Exempt Impact of Special Items	122	14	-23	310	32
Normalized Income After Tax	121	99	262	-28	701
Normalized Income Avail to Common	121	134	267	116	593
Basic Normalized EPS	1.15	1.28	2.56	1.13	5.88
Diluted Normalized EPS	1.15	1.26	2.56	1.13	5.83

Balance Sheet

	2019	2018	2017	2016	2015
Assets					
Cash	1,345	1,203	--	--	--
Cash & Equivalents	7	201	2,269	1,347	1,127
Short Term Investments	812	1,144	720	608	703
Cash and Short Term Investments	2,164	2,547	2,989	1,955	1,830
Trade Accounts Receivable, Gross	476	130	214	267	501
Provision for Doubtful Accounts	-1	-1	-2	0	0
Trade Accounts Receivable, Net	659	586	386	473	541
Notes Receivable - Short Term	24	0	20	15	1
Other Receivables	30	26	12	22	19
Total Receivables, Net	712	613	419	511	561
Inventory - Finished Goods	295	252	123	302	309
Inventory - Work in Progress	60	41	14	13	20
Inventory - Raw Materials	88	94	36	48	51
Total Inventory	444	388	172	363	380
Prepaid Expenses	186	150	73	77	75
Restricted Cash - Current	14	20	11	37	73
Other Current Assets	80	142	168	844	426
Other Current Assets, Total	94	161	179	881	499
Total Current Assets	3,600	3,860	3,833	3,788	3,346
Buildings	713	617	473	433	461
Land/Improvements	14	14	8	8	12
Machinery/Equipment	2,437	1,826	1,059	1,444	1,825
Construction in Progress	243	406	641	93	38
Other Property/Plant/Equipment	836	521	609	630	382
Property/Plant/Equipment - Gross	4,243	3,384	2,790	2,608	2,718
Accumulated Depreciation	-1,439	-1,319	-1,219	-1,531	-1,340
Property/Plant/Equipment - Net	2,804	2,065	1,572	1,078	1,378
Goodwill, Gross	408	408	--	--	--
Accumulated Goodwill Amortization	-393	-393	--	--	--
Goodwill, Net	14	14	14	14	85
Intangibles, Gross	112	112	145	145	121
Accumulated Intangible Amortization	-48	-37	-65	-57	-11
Intangibles, Net	65	74	80	88	110
Long Term Investments	3	3	220	235	400
Note Receivables - Long Term	22	35	63	66	35
Deferred Charges	0	27	27	27	1,134
Deferred Income Tax - Long Term Asset	131	78	51	255	358
Restricted Cash - Long Term	304	318	425	371	334
Other Long Term Assets	574	647	580	902	137
Total Assets	7,516	7,121	6,865	6,824	7,316
Liabilities					
Accounts Payable	218	233	120	149	338
Accrued Expenses	705	414	338	223	371
Notes Payable/Short Term Debt	0	0	0	0	0
Current Portion of Long-Term Debt/Capital Liabili	18	6	13	28	38
Customer Advances	323	130	82	309	18
Income Taxes Payable	17	21	20	13	1
Other Payables	--	--	--	--	29
Other Current Liabilities	37	42	78	187	166
Other Current Liabilities, Total	378	193	179	508	214
Total Current Liabilities	1,318	845	650	908	961
Total Long Term Debt	454	461	424	187	251
Total Debt	472	467	437	215	289
Other Liabilities, Total	647	602	692	511	556
Total Liabilities	2,419	1,909	1,766	1,606	1,768
Shareholder Equity					
Common Stock	0	0	0	0	0
Additional Paid-In Capital	2,849	2,825	2,799	2,765	2,743
Retained Earnings (Accumulated Deficit)	2,327	2,442	2,297	2,463	2,790
Unrealized Gain (Loss)	-5	11	68	65	87
Cumulative Translation Adjustment	-73	-66	-65	-77	-70
Other Comprehensive Income	-1	1	-1	2	-2
Other Equity, Total	-74	-65	-66	-75	-71
Total Equity	5,097	5,212	5,099	5,218	5,548
Total Liabilities & Shareholders' Equity	7,516	7,121	6,865	6,824	7,316
Total Common Shares Outstanding	105	105	104	104	102
Treasury Shares-Common Primary Issue	0	0	0	0	0

Cash Flows

	2019	2018	2017	2016	2015
Cash From Operating Activities					
Cash Taxes Paid, Supplemental	8	-49	169	-60	-13
Accounts Receivable	-74	-202	86	93	-340
Inventories	-84	-257	213	96	114
Prepaid Expesnes	-35	-53	27	10	-39
Other Assets	8	38	980	-612	-866
Accounts Payable	0	96	-47	-192	144
Accrued Expenses	401	101	-261	183	-146
Changes in Working Capital	166	-278	1,172	266	-312
Total Cash from Operations	174	-327	1,341	207	-325
Plus: Cash From Investing Activities					
Capital Expenditures	-669	-740	-514	-229	-166
Acquisition of Business	--	--	--	-10	0
Sale of Fixed Assets	0	248	0	292	0
Sale/Maturity of Investment	1,487	1,185	468	529	411
Purchase of Investments	-1,177	-1,369	-581	-423	-556
Other Investing Cash Flow	-3	-6	0	-13	156
Other Investment Cash Flow Items, Total	306	57	-112	374	10
Total Cash from Investing	-362	-683	-627	145	-156
Plus: Cash From Financing Activities					
Financing Cash Flow Items	-15	-17	6	-21	-39
Long Term Debt Issued	120	291	215	577	191
Long Term Debt Reduction	-30	-19	-29	-693	-51
Long Term Debt, Net	90	272	186	-116	140
Issue (Retirement) of Debt, Net	90	272	186	-116	140
Total Cash from Financing	75	255	192	-136	101
Equals: Increase In Cash					
Foreign Exchange Effects	-3	-14	9	-6	-19
Net Change in Cash	-116	-768	915	209	-399
Net Cash - Begin Balance/Reserved for Future Use	1,563	2,330	1,416	1,207	1,607
Net Cash - End Balance/Reserved for Future Use	1,447	1,563	2,330	1,416	1,207
Depreciation, Supplemental	205	131	115	231	258
Cash Taxes Paid, Supplemental	8	-49	169	-60	-13

Quarterly Statements
Income Statement

	Q3 2020	Q2 2020	Q1 2020	Q4 2019	Q3 2019
Revenue & Gross Profit					
Total Revenue	928	642	532	1,399	547
Operating Expenses					
Cost of Revenue, Total	635	505	442	1,066	408
Selling/Gen/Admin Expense	57	55	58	55	66
Labor & Related Expense	6	3	5	8	6
Sell/Gen/Admin Expenses, Total	63	58	63	63	72
Research & Development	23	22	26	25	25
Restructuring Charge	--	--	--	0	--
Litigation	0	6	--	363	--
Unusual Expense (Income)	0	6	--	363	--
Total Operating Expense	720	592	530	1,517	506
Operating Income					
Total Operating Income	207	51	2	-118	41
Non-Operating Income & Expenses					
Interest Expense, Non-Operating	-12	-4	-5	-5	-5
Interest Capital, Non-Operating	1	0	0	0	0
Interest Expense, Net Non-Operating	-11	-3	-4	-5	-5
Interest Income, Non-Operating	2	4	9	10	11
Investment Income, Non-Operating	-2	-1	-3	1	1
Interest/Investment Income, Non-Operating	0	2	7	10	12
Other Non-Operation Income (Expense)	-3	-3	-2	22	-3
Other, Net	-3	-3	-2	22	-3
Income Before Tax	193	47	2	-90	46
Income Taxes					
Provision for Income Taxes	38	10	-89	-31	15
Net Income After Taxes	155	37	91	-59	31
Minority Interest & Equity in Affiliates					
Equity in Affiliates	0	0	0	0	0
Net Income Before Extra Items	155	37	91	-59	31
Net Income					
Net Income	155	37	91	-59	31
Adjustments to Net Income					
Income Available to Common Excl. Extra. Items	155	37	91	-59	31
Income Available to Common Incl. Extra. Items	155	37	91	-59	31
EPS Reconciliation					
Basic/Primary Weighted Average Shares	106	106	106	105	105
Basic/Primary EPS Excl. Extra. Items	1.46	0.35	0.86	-0.56	0.29
Basic/Primary EPS Incl. Extra. Items	1.46	0.35	0.86	-0.56	0.29
Diluted Weighted Average Shares	107	106	106	105	106
Diluted EPS Excl. Extra. Items	1.45	0.35	0.85	-0.56	0.29
Diluted EPS Incl. Extra. Items	1.45	0.35	0.85	-0.56	0.29
Common Stock Dividends					
DPS - Common Stock Primary Issue	0	0	0	--	0
Gross Dividend - Common Stock	--	--	--	0	0
Pro Forma Net Income					
Pro Forma Net Income	--	--	--	--	--
Supplemental Items					
Interest Expense, Supplemental	11	3	11	8	10
Interest Capitalized, Supplemental	-1	0	0	0	0
Depreciation, Supplemental	57	55	54	53	49
Normalized Income					
Total Special Items	0	6	--	363	--
Normalized Income Before Tax	193	53	2	273	46
Effect of Special Items on Income Taxes	0	1	--	127	--
Income Tax Exempt Impact of Special Items	38	12	-89	96	15
Normalized Income After Tax	155	41	91	177	31
Normalized Income Avail to Common	155	42	91	177	31
Basic Normalized EPS	1.46	0.39	0.86	1.67	0.29
Diluted Normalized EPS	1.45	0.39	0.85	1.67	0.29

Balance Sheet

	Q3 2020	Q2 2020	Q1 2020	Q4 2019	Q3 2019
Assets					
Cash	1,277	1,052	929	1,345	872
Cash & Equivalents	0	0	0	7	7
Short Term Investments	354	494	579	812	662
Cash and Short Term Investments	1,631	1,547	1,509	2,164	1,541
Trade Accounts Receivable, Gross	311	356	416	476	369
Provision for Doubtful Accounts	-3	-4	-5	-1	-2
Trade Accounts Receivable, Net	307	352	411	659	532
Notes Receivable - Short Term	0	0	0	24	23
Other Receivables	3	4	29	30	28
Total Receivables, Net	310	355	441	712	584
Inventory - Finished Goods	--	--	--	295	--
Inventory - Work in Progress	--	--	--	60	--
Inventory - Raw Materials	--	--	--	88	--
Total Inventory	568	518	480	444	577
Prepaid Expenses	204	204	197	186	205
Restricted Cash - Current	2	51	48	14	32
Discontinued Operations - Current Assets	35	--	--	--	--
Other Current Assets	51	55	73	80	104
Other Current Assets, Total	87	107	121	94	137
Total Current Assets	2,800	2,731	2,748	3,600	3,043
Buildings	710	719	715	713	708
Land/Improvements	14	14	14	14	14
Machinery/Equipment	2,102	2,057	2,169	2,437	2,166
Construction in Progress	468	403	320	243	406
Other Property/Plant/Equipment	680	923	845	836	896
Property/Plant/Equipment - Gross	3,974	4,116	4,063	4,243	4,190
Accumulated Depreciation	-1,106	-1,089	-1,187	-1,439	-1,421
Property/Plant/Equipment - Net	2,868	3,027	2,876	2,804	2,768
Goodwill, Gross	408	408	408	408	408
Accumulated Goodwill Amortization	-393	-393	-393	-393	-393
Goodwill, Net	14	14	14	14	14
Intangibles, Gross	114	114	114	112	112
Accumulated Intangible Amortization	-56	-53	-50	-48	-45
Intangibles, Net	58	61	64	65	67
Long Term Investments	3	3	3	3	3
Note Receivables - Long Term	25	26	23	22	21
Deferred Charges	--	--	--	0	0
Deferred Income Tax - Long Term Asset	210	205	214	131	66
Total Assets	6,985	7,073	6,949	7,516	7,055
Liabilities					
Accounts Payable	154	159	174	218	218
Accrued Expenses	290	322	301	705	369
Notes Payable/Short Term Debt	0	0	0	0	0
Current Portion of Long-Term Debt/Capital Liabili	40	77	82	18	28
Customer Advances	116	131	137	323	93
Income Taxes Payable	32	17	8	17	15
Discontinued Operations	13	--	--	--	--
Other Current Liabilities	86	41	30	37	37
Other Current Liabilities, Total	246	189	176	378	145
Total Current Liabilities	731	747	732	1,318	761
Total Long Term Debt	220	388	391	454	452
Total Debt	261	465	472	472	480
Other Liabilities, Total	638	711	657	647	659
Total Liabilities	1,589	1,846	1,781	2,419	1,872
Shareholder Equity					
Common Stock	0	0	0	0	0
Additional Paid-In Capital	2,856	2,849	2,844	2,849	2,836
Retained Earnings (Accumulated Deficit)	2,600	2,445	2,408	2,327	2,386
Unrealized Gain (Loss)	16	10	-2	-5	32
Cumulative Translation Adjustment	-73	-76	-81	-73	-73
Other Equity, Total	-75	-77	-81	-74	-72
Total Equity	5,396	5,227	5,169	5,097	5,182
Total Liabilities & Shareholders' Equity	6,985	7,073	6,949	7,516	7,055
Total Common Shares Outstanding	106	106	106	105	105
Treasury Shares-Common Primary Issue	0	0	0	0	0

Cash Flows

	Q3 2020	Q2 2020	Q1 2020	Q4 2019	Q3 2019
Cash From Operating Activities					
Cash Taxes Paid, Supplemental	9	-9	-9	8	-25
Accounts Receivable	330	303	243	-74	52
Inventories	-142	-80	-49	-84	-224
Prepaid Expesnes	8	14	-13	-35	-29
Other Assets	152	-90	-106	8	-235
Accounts Payable	-58	-44	-38	0	-1
Accrued Expenses	-734	-640	-609	401	-184
Changes in Working Capital	-158	-349	-495	166	-583
Total Cash from Operations	-149	-357	-505	174	-607
Cash From Investing Activities					
Capital Expenditures	-327	-221	-113	-669	-511
Sale of Fixed Assets	--	--	--	0	0
Sale/Maturity of Investment	1,100	857	629	1,487	1,121
Purchase of Investments	-643	-541	-406	-1,177	-668
Other Investing Cash Flow	-14	-14	-14	-3	3
Other Investment Cash Flow Items, Total	444	302	209	306	456
Total Cash from Investing	116	81	96	-362	-55
Cash From Financing Activities					
Financing Cash Flow Items	-14	-14	-13	-15	-15
Long Term Debt Issued	140	0	0	120	107
Long Term Debt Reduction	-225	-9	0	-30	-11
Long Term Debt, Net	-84	-9	0	90	97
Issue (Retirement) of Debt, Net	-84	-9	0	90	97
Total Cash from Financing	-98	-23	-13	75	82
Equals: Increase In Cash					
Foreign Exchange Effects	1	0	-6	-3	-7
Net Change in Cash	-130	-299	-428	-116	-587
Net Cash - Begin Balance/Reserved for Future Use	1,447	1,447	1,447	1,563	1,563
Net Cash - End Balance/Reserved for Future Use	1,317	1,148	1,019	1,447	976
Depreciation, Supplemental	173	114	56	205	150
Cash Taxes Paid, Supplemental	9	-9	-9	8	-25

First Solar financial reports taken from Charles Schwab's Website. (Charles Schwab | A modern approach to investing & retirement, n.d.)

TNK/FRO

Both of these companies, TK Tankers Ltd. and Frontline Ltd., ship crude oil over the ocean in their ships. This is a business I did not understand and still do not understand very well. I did not try to think of the companies 5 years down the road, I simply bought them because they were cheap. **DO NOT INVEST IN COMPANIES YOU DO NOT UNDERSTAND.** I invested in both companies at the beginning of 2017. They were cheap stocks in terms of Book Value. They were selling for less than their assets subtracted by their liabilities. Looking at the Balance sheets below you can see that at the end of 2016 TNK had around $2 Billion in Assets and $1 Billion in Liabilities, so its book value was around $1 Billion. This company was selling for only $380 Million, meaning its PB ratio was roughly .4. You could buy a 1-Billion-dollar company for $380 Million. TNK certainly sounds like a tempting investment.

FRO was the same thing, at the end of 2016 they had around $3 Billion in assets and $1.5 Billion in Liabilities. I would subtract the $250 Million in goodwill they had, so you could say the company's assets are worth around $1.25 Billion. In 2017, FRO was selling for around $1.25 Billion so it wasn't a steal, but it was still around book value. I invested a decent amount of money in these companies. I had no idea what to expect for earnings and did not really care. I figured I bought a cheap company and should hold on to them. Over the next few years these companies lost money in 2017 and 2018 but made a small profit in 2019. I bought TNK for around $18 a share and FRO for a little over $7 a share in early 2017 (adjusting for a stock split). Four years later both companies are selling for less than I bought them. TNK is selling for less than $12 a share and FRO is selling for less than $7. I sold them after only a little while for small losses in each one. However, if someone would have held on to these companies until the beginning of 2020, they could have made a decent profit: TNK sold for a high of $24.89, a gain of 33% plus dividends. FRO sold for $13.18, a gain of 85% plus dividends.

These are companies like what Warren Buffett used to buy. He calls them cigar butts, meaning you find a dirty cigarette on the ground and you light it up and get one good puff out of it. With these types of companies, you buy them cheap and with some good news people might get excited, giving you one good puff before selling at a decent profit. Sometimes this works. However, Buffett has learned that "It's far better to buy a wonderful company at a fair price than a fair company at a wonderful price." – Warren Buffett (qtd. in Fox, 2019). It is better to buy companies like Apple at a decent price than companies like TNK and FRO at an excellent price.

I have purchased a handful of companies like this and have made a decent profit. However, as I learned more from Buffett and Munger, I realized I was wasting time with average or below average companies just because they were cheap.

Here are the TNK and FRO statements:
(Values are in millions except for per share data)

TNK Statements
Income Statement

	2019	2018	2017	2016	2015
Revenue & Gross Profit					
Total Revenue	944	776	431	551	535
Operating Expenses					
Cost of Revenue, Total	654	610	283	296	231
Selling/Gen/Admin Expense	36	39	32	33	30
Labor & Related Expense	1	1	1	--	--
Sell/Gen/Admin Expenses, Total	36	40	33	33	30
Depreciation/Amortization	124	119	100	104	74
Restructuring Charge	0	1	0	0	7
Unusual Expense (Income)	6	1	13	21	6
Loss (Gain)/Sale Assets (Operations)	6	0	13	21	-1
Total Operating Expense	820	769	430	454	341
Operating Income					
Total Operating Income	124	7	1	97	194
Non-Operating Income & Expenses					
Interest Expense, Net Non-Operating	-65	-59	-31	-30	-17
Interest Income, Non-Operating	1	1	1	0	0
Investment Income, Non-Operating	2	7	-24	7	10
Interest/Investment Income, Non-Operating	3	8	-23	7	10
Other Non-Operation Income (Expense)	0	0	0	-6	-3
Other, Net	0	0	0	-6	-3
Income Before Tax	61	-43	-53	68	184
Income Taxes					
Provision for Income Taxes	20	9	5	--	--
Net Income After Taxes	41	-53	-58	68	184
Minority Interest & Equity in Affiliates					
Net Income Before Extra Items	41	-53	-58	68	184
Net Income					
Net Income	41	-53	-58	68	184
Adjustments to Net Income					
Income Available to Common Excl. Extra. Items	41	-53	-58	68	184
Income Available to Common Incl. Extra. Items	41	-53	-58	68	184
EPS Reconciliation					
Basic/Primary Weighted Average Shares	34	34	23	21	18
Basic/Primary EPS Excl. Extra. Items	1.23	-1.57	-2.48	3.19	10.21
Basic/Primary EPS Incl. Extra. Items	1.23	-1.57	-2.48	3.19	10.21
Diluted Weighted Average Shares	34	34	23	21	18
Diluted EPS Excl. Extra. Items	1.23	-1.57	-2.48	3.19	10.17
Common Stock Dividends					
DPS - Common Stock Primary Issue	--	0.03	0.96	2.4	1.92
Gross Dividend - Common Stock	0	8	21	28	34
Pro Forma Net Income					
Pro Forma Net Income	--	--	--	--	--
Supplemental Items					
Interest Expense, Supplemental	65	59	31	30	17
Depreciation, Supplemental	122	116	97	104	74
Normalized Income					
Total Special Items	6	1	13	21	6
Normalized Income Before Tax	67	-42	-40	88	190
Effect of Special Items on Income Taxes	2	0	5	0	0
Income Tax Exempt Impact of Special Items	22	10	10	0	0
Normalized Income After Tax	45	-52	-50	88	190
Normalized Income Avail to Common	45	-52	-50	88	190
Basic Normalized EPS	1.34	-1.55	-2.12	4.16	10.54
Diluted Normalized EPS	1.34	-1.55	-2.12	4.15	10.5

Balance Sheet

	2019	2018	2017	2016	2015
Assets					
Cash and Short Term Investments	89	55	71	94	96
Trade Accounts Receivable, Net	96	74	35	58	91
Other Receivables	1	40	49	49	67
Total Receivables, Net	96	114	84	107	158
Inventories - Other	50	--	--	--	--
Total Inventory	50	--	--	--	--
Prepaid Expenses	10	34	19	21	24
Restricted Cash - Current	3	2	2	1	1
Discontinued Operations - Current Assets	65	--	0	34	--
Other Current Assets	107	21	1	1	--
Other Current Assets, Total	176	23	3	35	1
Total Current Assets	421	226	177	258	280
Machinery/Equipment	1,760	1,896	2,250	2,065	2,159
Other Property/Plant/Equipment	690	593	253	--	--
Property/Plant/Equipment - Gross	2,451	2,489	2,503	2,065	2,159
Accumulated Depreciation	-681	-606	-537	-459	-391
Property/Plant/Equipment - Net	1,770	1,884	1,966	1,605	1,768
Goodwill, Net	2	8	8	8	--
Intangibles, Gross	16	--	--	--	--
Accumulated Intangible Amortization	-13	--	--	--	--
Intangibles, Net	3	12	15	18	30
Long Term Investments	28	26	25	71	87
Restricted Cash - Long Term	3	3	3	--	--
Other Long Term Assets	2	3	4	5	5
Total Assets	2,229	2,161	2,197	1,964	2,169
Liabilities					
Accounts Payable	71	11	8	14	17
Accrued Expenses	76	40	35	28	62
Notes Payable/Short Term Debt	50	0	0	0	0
Current Portion of Long-Term Debt/Capital Liabili	69	127	174	171	174
Customer Advances	--	0	1	4	3
Other Payables	2	19	20	36	27
Other Current Liabilities	12	0	0	2	8
Other Current Liabilities, Total	14	19	20	43	37
Total Current Liabilities	280	198	237	256	290
Capital Lease Obligations	389	354	142	--	--
Total Long Term Debt	906	984	927	762	991
Total Debt	1,024	1,111	1,101	933	1,165
Other Liabilities, Total	54	33	27	14	12
Total Liabilities	1,240	1,214	1,191	1,032	1,292
Shareholder Equity					
Common Stock	34	1,296	1,295	1,103	1,095
Additional Paid-In Capital	1,264	--	--	--	--
Retained Earnings (Accumulated Deficit)	-308	-349	-288	-183	-217
Other Equity	--	--	0	12	0
Other Equity, Total	--	--	0	12	0
Total Equity	990	947	1,007	933	877
Total Liabilities & Shareholders' Equity	2,229	2,161	2,197	1,964	2,169
Shares Outstanding-Common Primary Issue	29	29	29	17	17
Shares Outstanding-Common Stock Issued 2	5	37	37	23	23
Total Common Shares Outstanding	34	66	66	40	40
Treasury Shares-Common Primary Issue	0	0	0	0	0
Treasury Shares-Common Issued 2	0	0	0	0	0

Cash Flow

	2019	2018	2017	2016	2015
Cash From Operating Activities					
Net Income	41	-53	-58	68	184
Depreciation/Depletion	124	119	100	104	74
Unusual Items	11	-1	12	11	-9
Equity in Net Earnings/Loss	-2	-1	25	-8	-12
Other Non-Cash Items	23	12	8	10	3
Non-Cash Items	31	10	46	13	-17
Cash Interest Paid, Supplemental	62	48	26	39	23
Changes in Working Capital	-79	-83	-7	21	-38
Total Cash from Operations	118	-7	80	207	202
Cash From Investing Activities					
Capital Expenditures	-12	-6	-5	-9	-848
Acquisition of Business	--	--	--	--	-46
Sale of Business	0	0	31	0	0
Sale of Fixed Assets	20	1	52	28	11
Sale/Maturity of Investment	0	1	0	--	1
Investment, Net	0	0	1	4	1
Purchase of Investments	--	--	--	--	0
Other Investment Cash Flow Items, Total	20	1	84	31	-33
Total Cash from Investing	8	-4	79	22	-881
Cash From Financing Activities					
Financing Cash Flow Items	0	0	0	-16	-32
Total Cash Dividends Paid	0	-8	-21	-47	-15
Sale/Issuance of Common	0	0	14	8	242
Common Stock, Net	0	0	14	8	242
Issuance (Retirement) of Stock, Net	0	0	14	8	242
Short Term Debt Issued	200	--	--	--	--
Short Term Debt Reduction	-150	--	--	--	--
Short Term Debt, Net	50	--	--	--	--
Long Term Debt Issued	121	323	386	906	689
Long Term Debt Reduction	-260	-318	-557	-1,142	-236
Long Term Debt, Net	-140	5	-171	-236	452
Issue (Retirement) of Debt, Net	-90	5	-171	-236	452
Total Cash from Financing	-90	-3	-178	-291	648
Equals: Increase In Cash					
Net Change in Cash	36	-15	-19	-62	-31
Net Cash - Begin Balance/Reserved for Future Use	61	76	95	157	188
Net Cash - End Balance/Reserved for Future Use	97	61	76	95	157
Depreciation, Supplemental	124	119	100	104	74
Cash Interest Paid, Supplemental	62	48	26	39	23

FRO statements
Income Statement

	2019	2018	2017	2016	2015
Revenue & Gross Profit					
Total Revenue	957	742	646	754	459
Operating Expenses					
Cost of Revenue, Total	552	508	395	281	174
Sell/Gen/Admin Expenses, Total	53	59	57	105	54
Depreciation/Amortization	118	123	142	141	53
Impair-Assets Held for use	0	0	277	62	--
Impair-Assets Held for Sale	--	0	0	7	11
Unusual Expense (Income)	-3	-10	275	72	-98
Loss (Gain)/Sale Assets (Operations)	-3	-10	-2	3	-109
Other Operating Expense, Total	-3	-20	-26	-15	--
Other, Net	-3	-20	-26	-15	--
Total Operating Expense	718	660	843	584	182
Operating Income					
Total Operating Income	240	83	-196	170	277
Non-Operating Income & Expenses					
Interest Expense, Net Non-Operating	-94	-93	-70	-57	-18
Interest Income, Non-Operating	2	1	1	0	0
Investment Income, Non-Operating	-7	1	0	4	-4
Interest/Investment Income, Non-Operating	-5	2	1	4	-4
Other Non-Operation Income (Expense)	0	1	1	0	0
Other, Net	0	1	1	0	0
Income Before Tax	140	-8	-264	118	256
Income Taxes					
Provision for Income Taxes	0	0	0	0	0
Net Income After Taxes	140	-8	-264	118	255
Minority Interest & Equity in Affiliates					
Minority Interest	0	0	-1	-1	30
Net Income Before Extra Items	140	-9	-265	117	286
Extraordinary Items					
Total Extraordinary Items	--	--	0	0	-131
Net Income					
Net Income	140	-9	-265	117	155
Adjustments to Net Income					
Income Available to Common Excl. Extra. Items	140	-9	-265	117	286
Income Available to Common Incl. Extra. Items	140	-9	-265	117	155
EPS Reconciliation					
Basic/Primary Weighted Average Shares	174	170	170	157	120
Basic/Primary EPS Excl. Extra. Items	0.81	-0.05	-1.56	0.75	2.38
Basic/Primary EPS Incl. Extra. Items	0.81	-0.05	-1.56	0.75	1.29
Diluted Weighted Average Shares	179	170	170	157	120
Diluted EPS Excl. Extra. Items	0.78	-0.05	-1.56	0.75	2.38
Diluted EPS Incl. Extra. Items	0.78	-0.05	-1.56	0.75	1.29
Common Stock Dividends					
DPS - Common Stock Primary Issue	0.5	--	0.3	1.05	0.25
Gross Dividend - Common Stock	0	0	42	164	191
Pro Forma Net Income					
Pro Forma Net Income	--	--	--	--	--
Supplemental Items					
Interest Expense, Supplemental	94	93	70	57	18
Depreciation, Supplemental	118	123	142	141	53
Normalized Income					
Total Special Items	-3	-10	275	72	-98
Normalized Income Before Tax	137	-18	11	189	157
Effect of Special Items on Income Taxes	0	-4	96	0	0
Income Tax Exempt Impact of Special Items	0	-3	96	1	0
Normalized Income After Tax	137	-15	-86	189	157
Normalized Income Avail to Common	137	-16	-86	188	187
Basic Normalized EPS	0.79	-0.09	-0.51	1.2	1.56
Diluted Normalized EPS	0.76	-0.09	-0.51	1.2	1.56

Balance Sheet

	2019	2018	2017	2016	2015
Assets					
Cash & Equivalents	174	66	104	202	265
Short Term Investments	11	20	39	18	23
Cash and Short Term Investments	185	87	143	221	288
Trade Accounts Receivable, Gross	66	60	56	55	59
Provision for Doubtful Accounts	-3	-6	-6	-6	-2
Trade Accounts Receivable, Net	79	62	55	54	68
Other Receivables	25	17	17	19	29
Total Receivables, Net	104	79	72	74	97
Total Inventory	67	69	62	38	26
Prepaid Expenses	11	8	6	6	4
Restricted Cash - Current	3	1	1	1	0
Other Current Assets	78	65	38	45	53
Other Current Assets, Total	81	66	39	46	53
Total Current Assets	448	308	322	384	467
Other Property/Plant/Equipment	496	141	359	607	706
Property/Plant/Equipment - Gross	496	141	359	607	706
Accumulated Depreciation	-66	-50	-107	-71	-12
Property/Plant/Equipment - Net	3,056	2,620	2,673	2,322	2,150
Goodwill, Gross	112	112	112	225	225
Goodwill, Net	112	112	112	225	225
Long Term Investments - Affiliate Comp.	5	6	--	--	--
Long Term Investments - Other	11	11	22	31	41
Long Term Investments	16	17	22	31	41
Deferred Charges	55	--	--	--	--
Other Long Term Assets	9	20	4	4	0
Total Assets	3,698	3,078	3,134	2,966	2,883
Liabilities					
Accounts Payable	13	22	12	4	10
Accrued Expenses	80	36	39	26	30
Notes Payable/Short Term Debt	0	0	0	0	0
Current Portion of Long-Term Debt/Capital Liabil	722	132	156	124	147
Income Taxes Payable	1	1	--	--	--
Other Payables	20	19	9	18	29
Other Current Liabilities	12	4	6	10	27
Other Current Liabilities, Total	33	24	15	28	55
Total Current Liabilities	848	214	222	183	242
Capital Lease Obligations	76	88	256	366	447
Total Long Term Debt	1,331	1,698	1,723	1,281	1,192
Total Debt	2,053	1,831	1,879	1,405	1,340
Minority Interest	0	0	0	0	0
Other Liabilities, Total	9	1	1	3	3
Total Liabilities	2,188	1,914	1,946	1,467	1,437
Shareholder Equity					
Common Stock	197	170	170	170	782
Additional Paid-In Capital	1,468	1,289	1,288	1,295	584
Retained Earnings (Accumulated Deficit)	-155	-295	-273	34	81
Other Equity, Total	0	0	2	1	0
Total Equity	1,510	1,164	1,187	1,500	1,446
Total Liabilities & Shareholders' Equity	3,698	3,078	3,134	2,966	2,883
Total Common Shares Outstanding	197	170	170	170	156
Treasury Shares-Common Primary Issue	0	0	0	0	0

Cash Flows

	2019	2018	2017	2016	2015
Cash From Operating Activities					
Net Income	140	-8	-264	118	124
Depreciation/Depletion	118	123	142	141	53
Discontinued Operations	--	--	--	--	125
Unusual Items	10	0	277	61	-95
Equity in Net Earnings/Loss	-2	0	0	0	-3
Other Non-Cash Items	18	-29	-26	-18	4
Non-Cash Items	26	-29	251	43	31
Cash Taxes Paid, Supplemental	0	0	1	1	0
Cash Interest Paid, Supplemental	91	81	57	53	18
Accounts Receivable	-22	0	2	15	-26
Inventories	2	-7	-24	-12	9
Prepaid Expesnes	-3	-2	0	-1	6
Other Assets	-6	-44	7	7	15
Accounts Payable	-9	10	7	-5	3
Accrued Expenses	36	-1	13	-3	-8
Changes in Working Capital	-4	-39	2	-16	0
Total Cash from Operations	280	46	130	286	207
Cash From Investing Activities					
Capital Expenditures	-196	-216	-714	-622	-787
Sale of Business	--	--	--	--	87
Sale of Fixed Assets	--	0	0	173	456
Sale/Maturity of Investment	0	18	27	0	0
Investment, Net	3	--	--	--	--
Purchase of Investments	0	-6	-46	0	--
Other Investing Cash Flow	2	5	10	53	-216
Other Investment Cash Flow Items, Total	5	17	-9	226	327
Total Cash from Investing	-191	-199	-723	-396	-459
Cash From Financing Activities					
Financing Cash Flow Items	-4	0	-3	-10	145
Total Cash Dividends Paid	-20	0	-51	-165	-39
Sale/Issuance of Common	98	0	0	98	0
Repurchase/Retirement Common	--	--	--	--	0
Common Stock, Net	98	0	0	98	0
Issuance (Retirement) of Stock, Net	98	0	0	98	0
Short Term Debt Issued	0	0	10	0	--
Short Term Debt, Net	0	0	10	0	
Long Term Debt Issued	146	299	673	356	660
Long Term Debt Reduction	-200	-183	-135	-232	-546
Long Term Debt, Net	-54	116	539	125	114
Issue (Retirement) of Debt, Net	-54	116	549	125	114
Total Cash from Financing	20	116	494	49	220
Equals: Increase In Cash					
Net Change in Cash	109	-37	-98	-62	-32
Net Cash - Begin Balance/Reserved for Future Us	68	105	203	265	236
Net Cash - End Balance/Reserved for Future Use	177	68	105	203	203
Depreciation, Supplemental	118	123	142	141	53
Cash Interest Paid, Supplemental	91	81	57	53	18
Cash Taxes Paid, Supplemental	0	0	1	1	0

TNK/FRO financial reports taken from Charles Schwab's Website. (Charles Schwab | A modern approach to investing & retirement, n.d.)

GURE

Here is my largest investment, Gulf Resources. GURE is a Chinese chemical company. It is another cigar butt company in the sense that it is "cheap" in terms of Book Value to Market Cap, and I do not plan to hold this company forever. However, I feel comfortable holding it for 5 plus years. GURE is different from the other companies above because I understand the business and can picture the company 5 years down the road. Here is what I think about the company.

GURE manufactures and sells Bromine and Crude Salt, they also have a chemical factory that uses the Bromine to create chemical products. GURE is selling for so cheap because for the last 3 years the company has been forced to shut down all their factories due to new environment regulations in China. The company's factories used to be in the middle of cities. The last 3 years they have had to demolish some factories and move to more secluded areas. They've also made major upgrades to some factories that were allowed to stay in place. This process has cost over 100 Million dollars so far, but the end is in sight.

Prior to shutting down their factories, GURE in 2015 had $162 Million in Revenue and $34 Million in Net Income. In 2016 they had $149 Million in Revenue and $36 Million in Net income. If they can get back to half of these levels, then the $45 Million market cap is extremely cheap. This would be an earnings yield of 40%. (18 Million divided by 45 equals .4 or 40%).

GURE has a total of 7 bromine and crude salt factories, and 4 of them have been approved to operate. The quarter from 6/1/2020 to 9/31/2020 was the first quarter in 3 years where they have had 4 factories running the entire quarter. The price of Bromine in China is near an all-time High, which is very good for GURE. China is an importer of Bromine, so it is easy for the company to find buyers. I am hoping the last 3 factories will get approved soon; there is a chance they do not ever get approved, but the company seems optimistic that they will get approved.

GURE just started building a chemical factory, and I am hoping it will be up and running early 2022. The chemical factory had the largest revenues and profit margins in 2015 for the company. GURE expects the profit margins to be even better when it is finished with the upgraded facility.

Here are GURE's 2015 Revenues by segment:

Bromine - $52 Million
Crude Salt - $10 Million
Chemical Products - $99 Million

Here is GURE's 2015 Net-Income by segment:

Bromine - $11 Million
Crude Salt - $1 Million
Chemical Products - $33 Million

With four bromine factories operating, GURE had $10 million in revenue in the third quarter (Q3) of 2020, very close to break even. The company expects to be profitable once these 4 factories are operating at full capacity. As GURE continues to build the chemical factory, they will continue to eat through cash. They expect to pay another $30 Million to build the factory. With $90 Million in cash and only $11 Million in liabilities, GURE has plenty of cash to fund this.

I have a couple concerns with GURE, the main one being the chance of fraud. The company is in China and does all its business in China, but their headquarters is in Nevada and they are listed in the Nasdaq. I think the chances of it being a fraud are low. GURE's independent accountant is Morison Cogen, and the company is registered with the PCAOB (Public Company Accounting Oversight Board), which makes me feel decent about it not being a fraud. While we cannot rule out fraud, a lot of people would have to be in on it or very ignorant to it. That is still a possibility.

Another concern is that GURE is very cheap but they do not issue a dividend or buyback shares. They issue a few shares every quarter, so I watch this to make sure they are not giving away too much of the company. Our current relationship with China is a risk, but I do not think it will have much effect long term. The fact that GURE is so small and in China means that the stock is very volatile.

Valuing a company like GURE is tricky because they do not pay dividends and they do not buy back shares, so I would value it extremely conservatively. When I bought this company, they had $366 Million in Assets and only $16 Million in liabilities, with $164 Million in cash. With good prospects in its business, I would take cash minus liabilities and give a conservative valuation of GURE at $148 Million on the low end. On the high end, I would say around $360 Million. I got this value from the fact that the company had a net income of $36 Million in 2016. If you wanted to earn 10% on your money, you would say the company was worth $360 Million. So, I believed the company was worth somewhere between $148-360 Million. When GURE is selling for $85 Million, this is a good deal on your money.

The value of a company changes as time goes on. In 2018 & 2019, all of GURE's factories were shut down except for a couple months. Then the second worst typhoon in Chinese history landed and shut down the factories again. During those two years GURE had only $14 million in revenue, with a negative cash flow of 109 Million dollars due to the cost of demolishing, upgrading, and building the factories. 2020 was better with the first 3 quarters having

$16 Million in revenue and negative $27 Million in cash flow.

Valuing GURE now, on the low end I would place it at $80 Million for cash minus liabilities and $264 Million for assets minus liabilities. I would add the thought that the company could profit $20-30ish Million in a year or two if everything goes well. The company is currently selling for $45 Million, still a deep discount on value. If I had simply bought this company at $80 Million and did not buy anymore, I would be down close to 50%. But instead I knew there was going to be trouble the next few years with no income, and the costs of getting the factories back up and running. GURE said that the smaller chemical companies were not going to be able to afford to make the required changes, so there would be less competition after the changes, which gave me more confidence to wait.

Anyway, as the stock dropped from $8 a share down to a low of $2.25 a share at the end of 2019, I just kept buying up shares, my average price bought per share was around $3.00. At $2.25 the company was selling for around $22 Million (Market Cap). At that time I thought the company was worth $95-260 Million; this is a steep discount and what we call a "margin of safety." So, by the end of 2019 I had put over 99% of my portfolio in GURE. (I had 1 share of BRK-B to be able to go to the annual meetings.) GURE was pretty much my entire Net worth. The stock went from $2.25 at the end of 2019 to $6.25 in July 2020—In just 7 months it gained 177%. I sold about half my shares at $6 a share simply because I had all my money in it. It dropped back down to $4 a share and I bought some more. I had the confidence to do this after all my mistakes and learning from my Apple mistake of not putting enough money into your best idea: "When it rains gold, put out the bucket, not the thimble" – Warren Buffett (qtd. in Crippen, 2010). Also, Charlie Munger talks about when he put all his capital into one company which gave me the courage to do this.

Below are GURE's Financial statements:
(Values are in millions except for per share data)

Income Statement

	2019	2018	2017	2016	2015
Revenue & Gross Profit					
Total Revenue	11	3	108	149	162
Operating Expenses					
Cost of Revenue, Total	5	1	63	95	111
Sell/Gen/Admin Expenses, Total	17	32	16	6	6
Research & Development	--	0	0	0	1
Depreciation/Amortization	12	--	--	--	--
Impair-Assets Held for use	0	33	18	0	1
Unusual Expense (Income)	0	52	18	1	1
Loss (Gain)/Sale Assets (Operations)	0	19	0	1	0
Other Operating Expense, Total	0	0	0	0	0
Other, Net	0	0	0	0	0
Total Operating Expense	34	86	96	102	117
Operating Income					
Total Operating Income	-23	-84	11	48	45
Non-Operating Income & Expenses					
Interest Expense, Net Non-Operating	0	0	0	0	0
Interest Income, Non-Operating	0	1	1	0	0
Interest/Investment Income, Non-Operating	0	1	1	0	0
Income Before Tax	-23	-83	12	48	45
Income Taxes					
Provision for Income Taxes	3	-13	4	12	11
Net Income After Taxes	-26	-70	8	36	34
Minority Interest & Equity in Affiliates					
Net Income Before Extra Items	-26	-70	8	36	34
Extraordinary Items					
Extraordinary Item	--	--	0	--	--
Total Extraordinary Items	--	--	0	--	--
Net Income					
Net Income	-26	-70	8	36	34
Adjustments to Net Income					
Income Available to Common Excl. Extra. Items	-26	-70	8	36	34
Income Available to Common Incl. Extra. Items	-26	-70	8	36	34
EPS Reconciliation					
Basic/Primary Weighted Average Shares	9	9	9	9	9
Basic/Primary EPS Excl. Extra. Items	-2.73	-7.47	0.85	3.91	3.77
Basic/Primary EPS Incl. Extra. Items	-2.73	-7.47	0.85	3.91	3.77
Diluted Weighted Average Shares	9	9	9	9	9
Diluted EPS Excl. Extra. Items	-2.73	-7.47	0.85	3.91	3.69
Diluted EPS Incl. Extra. Items	-2.73	-7.47	0.85	3.91	3.69
Common Stock Dividends					
DPS - Common Stock Primary Issue	--	--	--	--	0
Gross Dividend - Common Stock	0	--	0	--	0
Pro Forma Net Income					
Pro Forma Net Income	--	--	--	--	--
Supplemental Items					
Interest Expense, Supplemental	0	0	0	0	0
Depreciation, Supplemental	14	17	20	25	29
Normalized Income					
Total Special Items	0	52	18	1	1
Normalized Income Before Tax	-23	-31	29	49	46
Effect of Special Items on Income Taxes	0	18	5	0	0
Income Tax Exempt Impact of Special Items	3	5	9	12	12
Normalized Income After Tax	-26	-36	20	37	35
Normalized Income Avail to Common	-26	-36	20	37	35
Basic Normalized EPS	-2.73	-3.86	2.14	4.01	3.85
Diluted Normalized EPS	-2.73	-3.86	2.14	4.01	3.77

Balance Sheet

	2019	2018	2017	2016	2015
Assets					
Cash and Short Term Investments	100	179	209	164	134
Trade Accounts Receivable, Net	5	0	30	52	50
Other Receivables	0	0	0	0	0
Total Receivables, Net	5	0	30	52	50
Inventory - Finished Goods	1	0	1	--	5
Inventory - Work in Progress	--	--	0	--	1
Inventory - Raw Materials	0	0	0	--	1
Inventories - Other	0	0	0	--	0
Total Inventory	1	0	1	6	7
Prepaid Expenses	1	8	2	0	0
Deferred Income Tax	--	--	--	0	0
Other Current Assets	--	--	--	--	0
Other Current Assets, Total	--	--	--	0	0
Total Current Assets	107	187	242	222	191
Buildings	60	61	68	--	69
Machinery/Equipment	235	161	201	--	195
Construction in Progress	1	7	0	--	0
Other Property/Plant/Equipment	25	8	11	--	14
Property/Plant/Equipment - Gross	321	237	280	--	277
Accumulated Depreciation	-166	-154	-184	--	-149
Property/Plant/Equipment - Net	155	83	96	109	129
Goodwill, Net	--	0	29	28	30
Deferred Charges	1	10	14	5	5
Deferred Income Tax - Long Term Asset	16	19	7	2	2
Total Assets	279	299	387	366	357
Liabilities					
Accounts Payable	--	--	0	--	9
Payable/Accrued	1	--	--	9	--
Accrued Expenses	1	0	0	--	0
Notes Payable/Short Term Debt	0	0	0	0	0
Current Portion of Long-Term Debt/Capital Liabil	0	0	0	0	0
Income Taxes Payable	1	1	1	4	5
Other Payables	0	1	1	--	1
Other Current Liabilities	4	0	1	1	1
Other Current Liabilities, Total	5	2	3	5	7
Total Current Liabilities	6	3	3	14	16
Total Long Term Debt	2	2	2	2	3
Total Debt	2	2	3	2	3
Other Liabilities, Total	8	--	--	--	--
Total Liabilities	16	5	6	16	19
Shareholder Equity					
Conv. Preferred Stock - Non Redeemable	0	0	0	0	--
Preferred Stock - Non Redeemable, Net	0	0	0	0	--
Common Stock	0	0	0	0	0
Additional Paid-In Capital	95	95	95	94	94
Retained Earnings (Accumulated Deficit)	184	210	280	272	236
Treasury Stock - Common	-1	-1	-1	-1	-1
Cumulative Translation Adjustment	--	-10	8	-16	9
Other Equity, Total	-15	-10	8	-16	9
Total Equity	263	294	382	349	338
Total Liabilities & Shareholders' Equity	279	299	387	366	357
Total Common Shares Outstanding	10	9	9	9	9
Treasury Shares-Common Primary Issue	0	0	0	0	0

Cash Flows

	2019	2018	2017	2016	2015
Cash From Operating Activities					
Net Income	-26	-70	8	36	34
Depreciation/Depletion	14	17	20	25	29
Deferred Taxes	3	-13	-4	0	0
Unusual Items	0	47	19	-1	-1
Other Non-Cash Items	0	5	2	1	1
Non-Cash Items	0	52	21	0	1
Cash Taxes Paid, Supplemental	0	0	11	12	11
Accounts Receivable	-5	30	26	-6	7
Inventories	-1	1	5	1	-1
Prepaid Expesnes	0	0	-1	0	0
Accrued Expenses	0	--	--	--	--
Payable/Accrued	0	0	-8	-1	-2
Changes in Working Capital	-6	31	18	-6	7
Total Cash from Operations	-15	17	63	55	70
Cash From Investing Activities					
Capital Expenditures	-61	-35	-18	-17	-23
Acquisition of Business	--	--	--	0	-66
Sale of Business	--	--	--	0	14
Sale of Fixed Assets	--	--	--	--	0
Other Investing Cash Flow	0	-1	-10	2	-1
Other Investment Cash Flow Items, Total	0	-1	-10	2	-53
Total Cash from Investing	-61	-36	-28	-15	-76
Cash From Financing Activities					
Repurchase/Retirement Common	--	--	--	0	0
Common Stock, Net	--	--	--	0	0
Issuance (Retirement) of Stock, Net	--	--	--	0	0
Long Term Debt Reduction	0	0	0	0	0
Long Term Debt, Net	0	0	0	0	0
Issue (Retirement) of Debt, Net	0	0	0	0	0
Total Cash from Financing	0	0	0	0	0
Equals: Increase In Cash					
Foreign Exchange Effects	-3	-11	11	-10	-7
Net Change in Cash	-79	-30	45	30	-13
Net Cash - Begin Balance/Reserved for Future Us	179	209	164	134	147
Net Cash - End Balance/Reserved for Future Use	100	179	209	164	134
Depreciation, Supplemental	14	17	20	25	29
Cash Taxes Paid, Supplemental	0	0	11	12	11

Gulf Resources financial reports taken from Charles Schwab's Website.
(Charles Schwab | A modern approach to investing & retirement, n.d.)

BIIB

BIIB, or Biogen Inc., is the last stock I will discuss. All investing is value investing, but BIIB was not a "value" investment in the sense that I bought it for more than the company's balance sheet value is worth. For that matter, I bought it at way more than its assets minus liabilities value. In today's market you are not going to find many opportunities like you could have found in the 1970s. To find companies you will have to value the business based on how much cash it will produce year over year. "The value of a business is the present value of its cash flows from today to judgment day." -Warren Buffett (qtd. in *IntrinsicValue*, n.d.). This investment strategy is more like investing in a company such as Apple, again looking at how much cash it will produce. As you can see, I repeated myself 3 times because it is an extremely important point.

First off, looking at the Balance sheet you will see the tangible Book Value of BIIB is around $5.5 Billion. Its current market cap is $42 Billion, so it is easy to see this company is not "cheap." However, this is not too bad for a drug company. Looking at this company, we need to value it like valuing a company like Apple. Here are some of my thoughts on it: BIIB is a drug company, and they are in the S&P 500. I really like the management of this company; they are very shareholder friendly. In 2019 they had revenues just above $14 Billion with net income of $5.8 Billion. With a market cap of only $42.5 Billion, BIIB is selling for less than 8 times earnings or a 12.5% earnings yield. This is very cheap compared to the 38 times earnings for the S&P 500, with its earnings yield of 2.63%. Also, compare to the 10 yr. treasury which is returning only 1.1%.

In 2019, BIIB's main products were:

Multiple Sclerosis Drugs:
Tecfedera - $4.4 Billion
Avonex/Plegridy - $2.1 Billion
Tysabri - $1.9 Billion

Spinal Muscular Atrophy Drugs:
Spinraza - $2 Billion

Biosimilars:
3 products for a total of $730 Million

Anti-CD20 Therapeutic Programs:
$2.3 Billion
I believe this a partnership in which they receive some
money from Rituxan, Hycela, Gayza.

A major upside with BIIB would be if their drug
Aducanumab can get approved by the FDA. It has been a
controversy because in phase 3 they ended up cancelling
the trials. But then later they said at a high enough dose the
drug does work. Aducanumab would be the first drug to
help slow down early Alzheimer's. Alzheimer's is a huge
problem in the world. 5.6 Million people have Alzheimer's
in the United States alone and 44 Million people in the
world have some form of Alzheimer's. As the world's
population continues to grow and get older, this number is
surely to rise. There is no medicine that helps delay early
Alzheimer's. If approved, Aducanumab would be the first.

BIIB also has many other drugs in the pipeline, but I
am not sure about their market potential. I am not an expert
by any means in these medications. However, I have read a
good deal and believe in the company. My concerns about
the company are that I do not understand all the science
behind the drugs, so I must keep a close eye on the sales of
the drugs. Also, it is looking like BIIB's current drugs have

reached their sales potential; 2020 revenue and profits will be very similar to 2019. Their highest selling drug, Tecfedera for multiple sclerosis, is going to take a big hit as the patent has run off and now generic brand names are coming out which will lower the price dramatically. However, if earnings do not grow but stay steady, BIIB should still be a solid long-term investment. The company bought back over $5 Billion of its stock in 2019 and it looks like they will buy more this year. At these prices, the value will really add up. Even if earnings deteriorate 50-60 percent, the investment should turn out satisfactory. BIIB just needs to keep innovating and coming out with new drugs every few years. This is a good "Margin of safety."

Given that BIIB is selling for $42 Billion, if BIIB continues to have a net income in the $5-6 Billion range and continues to buy back $5-6 Billion in shares each year, you could expect an 11-14% return, and that is just if they can have steady revenues and profits. I got these numbers by dividing $5 Billion in repurchases by $42 Billion in market cap to get 11%, and dividing $6 Billion by $42 Billion to get 14%. As stated above, even if earnings drop 50% the returns would be between 5.5-7%. That is still a good investment compared to the 1% 10 yr. treasury bond and the 2.6% earnings yield form the S&P 500 at its current 38 times earnings.

I would not invest a lot of my capital into a company like BIIB. I would probably limit my investment to around 10-20% of my capital because I just do not understand all the science and the value of each of its patents. Nor can I fully estimate the earnings possibilities of all the drugs in the pipeline. However, I do understand that this is a business that earns a good return on capital, and the management has the best interest of shareholders in mind by buying back a lot of shares of stock. But I must watch the sales and earnings of these drugs very carefully.

What also gives me confidence in BIIB is that Berkshire Hathaway owns this company. Warren Buffett probably did not buy this company; it was likely one of the two investment managers inside Berkshire who also pick their own investments. They work with much smaller sums than Warren. However, knowing one of them invested a couple hundred million dollars into this company makes me think I am on the right track.

Since writing this, Biogen reported their earnings. Their revenues were down $1 Billion from the 2019 year, and Net income was down $1.9 Billion. Going into 2021, the company predicted earnings of $17 to $18.50 a share. With 152 Million shares, this puts the earnings around $2.5 Billion to $2.8 Billion. This is a significant drop from $5.8 Billion in 2019. However, earnings of $17 a share with a share price of $264 puts the PE Ratio at 15 with earnings yield of over 6%. With the 10-yr treasury at 1% and the S&P at 38 times earnings, earnings yield of only 2.6%, BIIB is still an attractive investment at current levels. I invested in this company for the long haul so I can take the fluctuations of earnings. I will continue to keep up with all the company's drugs and patents. Naturally, I will start to question the company if I stop believing in the management and its relationship with shareholders. So far, they have been excellent to shareholders.

Below are the company's financial statements:
(Values are in millions except for per share data)

Income Statement

	2019	2018	2017	2016	2015
Revenue & Gross Profit					
Total Revenue	14,378	13,453	12,274	11,449	10,764
Operating Expenses					
Cost of Revenue, Total	1,955	1,816	1,630	1,479	1,240
Selling/Gen/Admin Expense	2,209	2,001	1,840	1,826	1,986
Labor & Related Expense	148	106	96	122	127
Sell/Gen/Admin Expenses, Total	2,357	2,106	1,936	1,948	2,113
Research & Development	2,273	2,597	2,254	1,973	2,013
Amortization of Intangibles	274	381	815	373	383
Depreciation/Amortization	274	381	815	373	383
Investment Income, Operating	242	185	112	10	0
Interest/Investment Income, Operating	242	185	112	10	0
Purchased R&D Written Off	0	113	120	--	--
Restructuring Charge	2	12	1	33	93
Litigation	--	0	0	455	--
Impair-Assets Held for use	216	366	--	12	--
Impair-Assets Held for Sale	--	--	--	--	0
Other Unusual Expense (In)	55	--	--	--	--
Unusual Expense (Income)	273	491	121	500	93
Loss (Gain)/Sale Assets (Operations)	--	--	--	0	0
Other Operating Expense, Total	-38	-12	63	15	31
Other, Net	-38	-12	63	15	31
Total Operating Expense	7,335	7,564	6,930	6,298	5,873
Operating Income					
Total Operating Income	7,043	5,889	5,344	5,150	4,891
Non-Operating Income & Expenses					
Interest Expense, Net Non-Operating	-187	-201	-251	-260	-96
Interest Income, Non-Operating	120	113	79	63	22
Investment Income, Non-Operating	205	110	-21	-1	-32
Interest/Investment Income, Non-Operating	325	222	57	63	-10
Other Non-Operation Income (Expense)	-54	-11	-22	-20	-19
Other, Net	-54	-11	-22	-20	-19
Income Before Tax	7,126	5,900	5,129	4,933	4,767
Income Taxes					
Provision for Income Taxes	1,158	1,402	1,285	1,237	1,162
Net Income After Taxes	5,968	4,498	3,844	3,696	3,606
Minority Interest & Equity in Affiliates					
Minority Interest	0	-43	-131	7	-46
Equity in Affiliates	-79	0	0	0	-13
Net Income Before Extra Items	5,889	4,454	3,713	3,703	3,547
Extraordinary Items					
Extraordinary Item	--	-24	-1,174	--	--
Total Extraordinary Items	--	-24	-1,174	--	--
Net Income					
Net Income	5,889	4,431	2,539	3,703	3,547
Adjustments to Net Income					
Income Available to Common Excl. Extra. Items	5,889	4,454	3,713	3,703	3,547
Income Available to Common Incl. Extra. Items	5,889	4,431	2,539	3,703	3,547
EPS Reconciliation					
Basic/Primary Weighted Average Shares	187	205	213	218	231
Basic/Primary EPS Excl. Extra. Items	31.47	21.74	17.46	16.95	15.37
Basic/Primary EPS Incl. Extra. Items	31.47	21.62	11.94	16.95	15.37
Dilution Adjustment	0	--	--	--	--
Diluted Weighted Average Shares	187	205	213	219	231
Diluted EPS Excl. Extra. Items	31.42	21.7	17.43	16.92	15.34
Diluted EPS Incl. Extra. Items	31.42	21.58	11.92	16.92	15.34
Common Stock Dividends					
DPS - Common Stock Primary Issue	--	--	--	0	0
Gross Dividend - Common Stock	0	0	0	0	0
Pro Forma Net Income					
Pro Forma Net Income	--	--	--	--	--
Supplemental Items					
Interest Expense, Supplemental	187	201	251	260	96
Interest Capitalized, Supplemental	-69	-54	-31	-13	-10
Depreciation, Supplemental	191	269	386	309	218
Normalized Income					
Total Special Items	273	491	121	500	93
Normalized Income Before Tax	7,399	6,390	5,250	5,433	4,861
Effect of Special Items on Income Taxes	44	90	0	125	23
Income Tax Exempt Impact of Special Items	1,202	1,492	1,285	1,363	1,184
Normalized Income After Tax	6,196	4,898	3,964	4,070	3,676
Normalized Income Avail to Common	6,117	4,855	3,833	4,077	3,618
Basic Normalized EPS	32.69	23.7	18.03	18.67	15.68
Diluted Normalized EPS	32.64	23.65	18	18.64	15.65

Balance Sheet

	2019	2018	2017	2016	2015
Assets					
Cash & Equivalents	2,914	1,225	1,574	2,327	1,308
Short Term Investments	1,562	2,313	2,115	2,569	2,121
Cash and Short Term Investments	4,476	3,538	3,689	4,895	3,429
Trade Accounts Receivable, Net	2,471	2,485	2,320	1,742	1,542
Total Receivables, Net	2,471	2,485	2,320	1,742	1,542
Inventory - Finished Goods	175	134	157	170	143
Inventory - Work in Progress	460	607	606	699	578
Inventory - Raw Materials	170	196	162	170	213
Inventories - Other	0	-7	-23	-38	-40
Total Inventory	804	930	903	1,002	893
Prepaid Expenses	--	--	658	817	--
Other Current Assets	631	688	305	276	837
Other Current Assets, Total	631	688	305	276	837
Total Current Assets	8,382	7,641	7,873	8,732	6,700
Buildings	935	1,377	1,294	1,232	1,202
Land/Improvements	118	145	141	138	75
Machinery/Equipment	1,643	2,057	1,975	1,853	1,727
Construction in Progress	2,084	1,759	1,276	659	441
Other Property/Plant/Equipment	485	62	55	61	73
Property/Plant/Equipment - Gross	5,265	5,399	4,742	3,941	3,518
Accumulated Depreciation	-1,591	-1,797	-1,559	-1,439	-1,330
Property/Plant/Equipment - Net	3,674	3,601	3,182	2,502	2,188
Goodwill, Net	5,758	5,706	4,633	3,669	2,664
Intangibles, Gross	8,409	7,727	8,265	7,742	7,646
Accumulated Intangible Amortization	-4,881	-4,607	-4,385	-3,934	-3,561
Intangibles, Net	3,527	3,120	3,880	3,808	4,085
Long Term Investments - Affiliate Comp.	580	681	--	--	--
Long Term Investments - Other	2,074	2,358	4,056	4,159	3,868
Long Term Investments	2,654	3,039	4,056	4,159	3,868
Deferred Charges	7	28	29	--	--
Deferred Income Tax - Long Term Asset	3,232	2,154	--	--	--
Other Long Term Assets	--	--	0	7	0
Total Assets	27,234	25,289	23,653	22,877	19,505
Liabilities					
Accounts Payable	531	371	396	280	267
Accrued Expenses	1,683	1,546	1,236	1,506	1,101
Notes Payable/Short Term Debt	0	0	0	0	0
Current Portion of Long-Term Debt/Capital Liabil	1,496	0	3	5	5
Customer Advances	--	--	--	--	56
Income Taxes Payable	71	64	68	232	209
Other Current Liabilities	1,083	1,316	1,665	1,397	940
Other Current Liabilities, Total	1,155	1,379	1,733	1,629	1,204
Total Current Liabilities	4,864	3,295	3,368	3,420	2,578
Capital Lease Obligations	--	--	0	16	18
Total Long Term Debt	4,459	5,937	5,935	6,513	6,522
Total Debt	5,955	5,937	5,938	6,517	6,526
Deferred Income Tax	2,811	1,636	123	93	125
Minority Interest	-4	-8	-15	-12	2
Pension Benefits - Underfunded	--	--	--	--	235
Other Long Term Liabilities	1,762	1,389	1,629	723	670
Other Liabilities, Total	1,762	1,389	1,629	723	906
Total Liabilities	13,891	12,249	11,040	10,737	10,132
Shareholder Equity					
Common Stock	0	0	0	0	0
Additional Paid-In Capital	0	0	98	0	0
Retained Earnings (Accumulated Deficit)	16,455	16,257	15,810	15,072	12,208
Treasury Stock - Common	-2,977	-2,977	-2,977	-2,612	-2,612
Unrealized Gain (Loss)	4	-4	-2	-11	-1
Cumulative Translation Adjustment	-140	-243	-176	-334	-196
Min. Pension Liability Adjustment	-33	-31	-37	-33	-38
Other Comprehensive Income	33	38	-105	58	10
Other Equity, Total	-139	-236	-317	-309	-223
Total Equity	13,343	13,040	12,613	12,140	9,373
Total Liabilities & Shareholders' Equity	27,234	25,289	23,653	22,877	19,505
Total Common Shares Outstanding	174	197	212	216	219
Treasury Shares-Common Primary Issue	24	24	24	23	23

Cash Flow Statement

	2019	2018	2017	2016	2015
Cash From Operating Activities					
Net Income	5,889	4,474	2,670	3,696	3,593
Depreciation/Depletion	681	1,017	1,081	683	600
Deferred Taxes	67	108	92	-175	-146
Unusual Items	55	--	--	--	--
Purchased R&D	0	113	120	0	0
Other Non-Cash Items	188	76	353	259	322
Non-Cash Items	243	189	473	259	322
Cash Taxes Paid, Supplemental	1,065	1,007	1,066	1,642	--
Cash Interest Paid, Supplemental	244	243	282	281	--
Accounts Receivable	6	-200	-668	-228	-2
Inventories	-19	-52	-95	-166	-174
Other Assets	--	-119	-77	59	-127
Accrued Expenses	240	466	-227	622	199
Changes in Working Capital	199	400	235	125	-450
Total Cash from Operations	7,079	6,188	4,551	4,587	3,919
Cash From Investing Activities					
Purchase/Acquisitions of Intangibles	-155	-3	-975	-112	-15
Capital Expenditures	-670	-886	-1,963	-728	-658
Acquisition of Business	-744	--	0	0	-199
Sale of Business	924	--	--	--	--
Sale/Maturity of Investment	6,486	9,174	5,566	7,379	4,063
Purchase of Investments	-5,253	-8,834	-5,355	-7,913	-6,865
Other Investing Cash Flow	-273	-1,500	-1,211	-1,223	-895
Other Investment Cash Flow Items, Total	1,140	-1,160	-1,000	-1,757	-3,895
Total Cash from Investing	471	-2,046	-2,963	-2,485	-4,554
Cash From Financing Activities					
Financing Cash Flow Items	8	-116	-454	-50	-145
Repurchase/Retirement Common	-5,868	-4,353	-1,365	-1,000	-5,000
Common Stock, Net	-5,868	-4,353	-1,365	-1,000	-5,000
Issuance (Retirement) of Stock, Net	-5,868	-4,353	-1,365	-1,000	-5,000
Long Term Debt Issued	--	--	0	0	5,931
Long Term Debt Reduction	0	-3	-561	-3	-2
Long Term Debt, Net	0	-3	-561	-3	5,928
Issue (Retirement) of Debt, Net	0	-3	-561	-3	5,928
Total Cash from Financing	-5,860	-4,472	-2,380	-1,053	783
Equals: Increase In Cash					
Foreign Exchange Effects	0	-19	39	-31	-46
Net Change in Cash	1,689	-349	-753	1,019	103
Net Cash - Begin Balance/Reserved for Future Us	1,225	1,574	2,327	1,308	1,205
Net Cash - End Balance/Reserved for Future Use	2,914	1,225	1,574	2,327	1,308
Depreciation, Supplemental	681	1,017	1,081	683	600
Cash Interest Paid, Supplemental	244	243	282	281	--
Cash Taxes Paid, Supplemental	1,065	1,007	1,066	1,642	--

Biogen financial reports taken from Charles Schwab's Website.
(Charles Schwab | A modern approach to investing & retirement, n.d.)

Post-Intelligent Investor Overview

After reading *The Intelligent Investor*, you will understand how to view stocks as businesses and not little symbols that move up and down. If you can understand this, you are on your way to becoming an efficient investor. You will also want to look for companies with PB ratios of less than 1 and PE ratios of less than 10. If you can find a group of companies with these characteristics and honest accounting, there is little chance you will lose money in the long run. But in today's markets it is going to be difficult to find businesses that meet these criteria. It is better to look for a great company selling at a decent price than a mediocre company at a great price. You need to study each company you're interested in and study their competitors as well. Only after careful research can you determine if you can value the company or not.

If you cannot value the company, do not worry about it and move on to the next one. If you can value the company, then give it a range of the company's business value or intrinsic value. Decide if the company is selling for less than you think it is worth. If so, then you can buy this company. Remember, a business's value is how much cash it is going to produce from now to judgment day. The company needs to distribute this cash back to you in the form of dividends, stock repurchases, and retained earnings to build a more competitive and profitable business. Always invest in your best idea. If you have an investment that will yield 10% a year, do not put money into your 10th best idea that you think will yield 2%.

Conclusion

Charlie Munger says when looking at a problem invert, always invert. This means if you want to figure out how to do something, think about how not to do it, then do not do those things.

What not to do in investing:

- **Do not buy a stock because it has gone up.**
- **Do not buy a stock because it has gone down (even though it is better than buying it when it has gone up).**
- **Do not listen to other people's advice online or on social media.**
- **Do not buy a company that is losing billions of dollars a year. Unless you are certain they will turn it around quick, which I doubt they will.**
- **Do not try to guess if the market is going to go up or down over the next day, month, or year.**
- **Do not listen to what you read on the internet or see on TV.**
- **Do not buy a stock just because you like or use their product.**
- **Do not invest in a company that has never made a sale (Obviously....... But I still lost money in one that did this).**
- **Do not buy a company that you do not understand.**
- **Do not buy a company with more liabilities than assets without great business prospects.**
- **Do not buy a company with dishonest managers.**
- **Do not buy a company that loses millions/billions of dollars a year with no prospects of a turnaround.**

- **Do not put money into your 10th best idea if your best idea is available.**
- **Do not put money into an investment that will return less than the S&P or the 10 yr. treasury.**
- **Do not buy a great company if the stock is too high.**
- **Do not buy a company just because its stock price is low.**
- **Do not let Mr. Market tempt you into buying companies that are too expensive and do not let him tempt you to sell companies when he thinks the world is ending.**
- **Do not buy a stock because the stock is going to split or has just split.**

After reading my book you are not yet ready to invest in stocks. You still need to read *The Intelligent Investor* and many other books. On top of that you need to read annual reports, and all information you can find on each company you are interested in. Again, if that does not sound like something you want to do, just invest monthly into the S&P 500 and become a millionaire one day. I know a lot of people cannot help themselves and are going to invest without reading anything, let alone reading more than this. My hope is that you will at least look at the financial statements and understand what the company does and where their profits come from. **Do not invest in companies that lose money every year and have no prospects for turning a profit.** Good luck out there, be honest and track your own performance. And if you have a money manager track their performance over a 3, 5, 10-year period. If they are underperforming the S&P 500, they are stealing from you. There is nothing wrong with simply getting the average of U.S businesses with the S&P 500; you will beat what most money managers would return to you. Good luck.

Further Reading

1. *The Intelligent Investor*, by Benjamin Graham

This is the Bible of investing. Written in 1949 by Warren Buffett's mentor, Buffett says that this is "By far the best book on investing ever written" (Morris, 2020). I must agree, before reading Graham's work I underperformed the market. Since then I have beaten the market.

2. *Poor Charlie's Almanack: The Wit and Wisdom of Charles T. Munger*, by Charles Munger

Written by Buffett's right-hand man, this is not necessarily a stock-picking book, but it will give you tons of worldly knowledge while being a very fun and easy read. It will make you a better investor and thinker. Charlie Munger is a genius.

3. *Warren Buffett and the Interpretation of Financial Statements*, by Mary Buffett and David Clark

This is a great book for beginners to learn the basic accounting terms in financial statements.

The rest of these books are not in any order, but I enjoyed them and would recommend them to any investor:

a) *Security Analysis*, **by Benjamin Graham & David L. Dodd**

b) *A Few Lessons for Investors and Managers from Warren Buffett*, **edited by Peter Bevelin**

c) *Tap Dancing to Work: Warren Buffett on Practically Everything*, **edited by Carol J. Loomis**

d) *Where Are The Customers' Yachts? Or a Good Hard Look at Wall Street*, by Fred Schwed

e) *Common Stocks and Uncommon Profits*, by Philip Fisher

f) *Stress Test: Reflections on Financial Crises*, by Tim Geithner

g) *The Outsiders*, by William Thorndike Jr.

i) *Business Adventures: Twelve Classic Tales from the World of Wall Street*, by John Brooks

j) *Jack: Straight from the Gut*, by Jack Welch

k) *Essays in Persuasion*, by John Maynard Keynes

l) *The Little Book of Common Sense Investing*, by Jack Bogle

m) *The Most Important Thing Illuminated*, by Howard Marks

n) *Dream Big*, by Cristiane Correa

o) *Take on the Street*, by Arthur Levitt

p) *Nuclear Terrorism: The Ultimate Preventable Catastrophe*, by Graham Allison

q) *The Clash of Cultures: Investment vs. Speculation*, by John Bogle

r) *Titan*, by Ron Chernow

s) *Sam Walton: Made in America*, by Sam Walton & John Huey

t) *First Billion is the Hardest*, by T. Boone Pickens

u) *Shoe Dog*, by Phil Knight

v) *The Essays of Warren Buffett: Lessons for Corporate America*, edited by Lawrence A. Cunningham

w) *A Few Lessons for Investors and Managers From Warren Buffett*, **by Peter Bevelin & Warren Buffet**

x) *Buffett: The making of an American Capitalist*, **by Roger Lowenstein**

y) *Money Game*, **by Adam Smith**

z) *SuperMoney*, **by Adam Smith**

References

10-k. (n.d.). SPYR, Inc. (SPYR). https://ir.spyr.com/annual-reports#document-12044-0001262463-16-000892

Buffet, W. (2013, Sept. 13). *Buffett explains intrinsic value – Warren buffet on investment.* Warren Buffet on Investment – Curated quotes, speeches and videos. https://warrenbuffettoninvestment.com/buffett-explains-intrinsic-value/

Charles Schwab: A modern approach to investing & retirement. (2021). https://www.schwab.com/

Clover, J. (2020, May 19). *Apple continues to top overall smartphone customer satisfaction index.* MacRumors. https://www.macrumors.com/2020/05/19/apple-smartphone-customer-satisfaction-index/

Crippen, A. (2010, Feb. 27). *Warren Buffett: "When it's raining gold, reach for a bucket."* CNBC. https://www.cnbc.com/id/35616702

DiLallo, M. (2013, Oct. 8). *3 reasons to buy LINN energy.* The Motley Fool. https://www.fool.com/investing/general/2013/10/08/3-reasons-to-buy-linn-energy.aspx

Fox, M. (2019, Sept. 19). *How to invest like Warren Buffett.* CNBC. https://www.cnbc.com/2019/09/19/heres-how-to-invest-like-warren-buffett.html

Graham, B. (1985). *The intelligent investor: A book of practical counsel.* HarperCollins.

Haque, M. E. (2020, July 7). *Invest in the business, not in the stock.* Value Research | Complete Guide to Mutual Funds, Investing in Stocks, Financial Planning. https://www.valueresearchonline.com/stories/23324/invest-in-the-business-not-in-the-stock/

Intrinsicvalue — Investment masters class. (n.d.). Investment Masters Class. https://mastersinvest.com/intrinsicvalue

Kim, T. (2018, Sept. 12). *Warren Buffett on why bubbles happen: People see neighbors 'dumber than they are' getting rich.* CNBC. https://www.cnbc.com/2018/09/12/warren-buffett-on-why-the-next-financial-crisis-is-unavoidable-greed.html

Mahomed, T. (2020, Feb. 24). *Warren Buffett is cheering the ongoing sell-off, saying investors 'should want the stock market to go down'.* markets.businessinsider.com. https://markets.businessinsider.com/news/stocks/warren-buffett-berkshire-hathaway-investors-should-want-stock-market-down-2020-2-1028930942

Mohamed, T. (2020, Aug. 20). Warren Buffett advised Airbnb CEO Brian Chesky to "get rich slow." *Business Insider.* https://markets.businessinsider.com/news/stocks/warren-buffett-airbnb-brian-chesky-get-rich-slow-ipo-filing-2020-8-1029520058

Morris, E. (2020, December 6). *The intelligent investor by Benjamin Graham book review.* Investopedia. https://www.investopedia.com/articles/07/ben_graham.asp

Munger, C. T. (2006). *Poor Charlie's Almanack: The wit and wisdom of Charles T. Munger* (3rd ed.). Donning Company Pub.

Owen, M. (2019, September 24). *Apple leads the entire US PC market in consumer satisfaction.* AppleInsider. https://appleinsider.com/articles/19/09/24/apple-leads-the-entire-us-pc-market-in-consumer-satisfaction

U.S. Securities and Exchange Commission. (n.d.). *10-k.* SEC.gov. https://www.sec.gov/Archives/edgar/data

/1326428/000132642816000071/linnform10-k2015.htm#sB45558D6C92E55BA7FE8D353FBC008E1

U.S. Securities and Exchange Commission.
(n.d.). *Compound interest calculator.*
Investor.gov. https://www.investor.gov/financial-tools-calculators/calculators/compound-interest-calculator

United States Securities and Exchange Commission.
(n.d.). *10-k.*
SEC.gov. https://www.sec.gov/Archives/edgar/data/1517681/000114420415057458/v420861_10k.htm#fin_003

Valuequotes — Investment masters class. (2021).
Investment Masters
Class. https://mastersinvest.com/valuequotes

SeekingAlpha. *The voting machine vs. the weighing machine.* (2019, June
19). https://seekingalpha.com/article/4182708-voting-machine-vs-weighing-machine

About the Author:

Maxx grew up on the west side of Washington State, later moving east to attend college at Washington State University. At WSU he earned a bachelor's degree in Mathematics, while also starting his investing career and passion for business. Although Maxx has spent nearly the past decade studying and investing in the stock market, he is also a teacher at heart. He has a Washington State teaching certificate and is a high-school mathematics teacher. His natural ability and love for teaching is what inspired him to write this book.

Maxx is an experienced investor. Like all experienced investors, he has made some mistakes. Thankfully, Maxx has learned from those mistakes, and he hopes that this book will help you avoid them as you begin your journey to investing.

About the Editor:

T.J. Carter, M.A., is an ESL teacher and English literature scholar. T.J. is currently studying library science at the University of Wisconsin—Milwaukee. As an aspiring investor, T.J. edited this book and simultaneously gained the knowledge to begin. T.J. hopes that by reading *Investing in Stocks for Beginners: The Knowledge Needed to Get Started and Avoid Rookie Mistakes* others will gain the same confidence and understanding that he did. Investing is not limited to those with large amounts of capital, nor is it limited to a particular age or demographic. Whether you are starting your first job or thinking about retirement, you can learn to invest. The world of investing may seem like an unknown forest, fraught with twists and turns. But so seems every journey when we first begin. Be bold, my friends, and let this book be your first map. The future lies before us. Take a deep breath, and turn the page. —T.J.

Made in the USA
Middletown, DE
26 December 2021